trippen

BRANDS A TO Z: TRIPPEN
Copyright © 2010 PAGE ONE PUBLISHING PTE LTD

Published in 2010 by
Page One Publishing Pte Ltd
20 Kaki Bukit View
Kaki Bukit Techpark II
Singapore 415956
Tel: [65] 6742 2088
Fax: [65] 6744 2088
enquiries@pageonegroup.com
www.pageonegroup.com

Design: **Beverly Chong and Huang Weiming**
Editor: **Wong She-reen**
Copy Editor: **Rachel Koh**
Typeset in ITC Slimbach

ISBN 978-981-245-943-5

Printed and bound by:
Dami Editorial & Printing Services Co. Ltd

trippen

CONTENTS

FOREWORD

Well-heeled:
Luxury Redefined

The words "real product" pop up often in a conversation about shoes with Angela
Spieth and Michael Oehler. Coming from an advertisement or a salesperson, the
expression might sound trite or worse, vacuous. When Oehler the master craftsman
and Spieth the design industry veteran spout it, however, they mean business, for
making an authentic, fairly-produced product is integral to the success of their label.
And while they are in the business of manufacturing shoes, their real interest is
in ideas, whether entrepreneurial initiatives, pattern innovation and development,
solutions to production problems or inspiration that turns into conceptual work.

The commitment to a real product stems also from ideas of honesty, fairness
and excellence, qualities both Trippen founders insist be present in every part
of the company they oversee. Yet, as shoemakers working primarily with leather,
their notions of luxury are not those shared by the mass market fashion houses.
To Trippen, if they're in the business of shoemaking, then shoes it is they sell.
Luxury shoes, but luxury defined differently. To them, a leather shoe handcrafted
from top-quality, traditionally tanned European leather handpicked for its specific
qualities is a genuine luxury product. A shoe made from leather that has a perfectly
even surface because it is covered with a layer of PUR, or polyurethane soft foam
(a common industry practice), assembled in a factory in Asia under less than
satisfactory conditions and eventually sold for astronomical prices to cover the
costs accrued not from skilled, fairly-paid labour but big-budget marketing, is not.

Oehler discusses the divide in more explicit terms, explaining that PUR is used,

> so that a unified structure is obtained and no blemishes are visible. As a result,
> real leather surfaces are a luxury, as nature is seldom free of flaws. In contrast,
> Trippen shoes show precisely where the barbed wire injured the cow or where
> mosquitoes plagued the elk.

Background image: From a trade fair invitation to view the autumn/winter 2009/2010 collections

In other words, Trippen shoes reflect an image of life and nature not in glossy Technicolour but ridden with blurry focus, scratches, imperfection. This lack of concealment is defined by Trippen as true luxury because it means paying higher prices for high-quality raw material since there are no cutting corners, or disguising a second-rate product under a camouflage. This paradigm of investing in quality is gaining ground in many design fields today but it was a mainstay of Trippen from the latter's inception, at a time when sustainable fashion was not yet adopted by Hollywood celebrities and mainstream fashion designers. Investing in high-quality raw material for a well-made product is straightforward and transparent, without any need for a complicated chain of hidden costs that the consumer has to bear. Simplicity is thus another kind of luxury. Spieth complements Oehler's vision: pronouncing the death of mediocre products masked by the glossy allure of big-budget advertising, she predicts that it is handicraft that will become the luxury of the 21st century due to its rarity, laboriousness, intricacy and time-consuming nature. This means handicraft will become extremely expensive, and will in turn lead to an intriguing phenomenon that is already seen even in the top fashion houses – the development of machinery that simulates the traits of handicraft production. Rather than representing a nostalgic return to an earlier, simpler time, the turn towards craft is a cultural cast into a technologically advanced postmodern culture with a sophisticated recognition of excellence in quality.

Calling what they do haute couture for shoes, Oehler and Spieth reveal another singular characteristic that sets Trippen apart: innovation in pattern development. It involves going against another currently predominant industry practice – the reliance on digitalised lasts produced anew, every season with every new collection, while only relatively small modifications are made to proportion or embellishment. This means a different last, a different heel height or toe shape – round, pointy or square, for example – every season, with new colours and new materials added, yet the underlying patterns cut to make the uppers – Oxfords, Derbies or wingtips, for example, each has a unique last – remain largely unaltered. In practice, this makes for a large amount of waste generated (since the old lasts will, presumably, be discarded once the season is over) as well as the consumption of a substantial amount of resources for the manufacture of new lasts for a new season.

Trippen marches to a different beat: Developing lasts that stay true to the human anatomical model, they keep to a single last for each collection, season after season, drawing completely new patterns and styles for the upper. This calls for true experimentation and breaking of new ground in shoe design, since fresh templates have to be generated based on the same foundations. Even the materials remain the same, supplemented by new colours every season. Moreover, a Trippen collection is not categorised by season, but a distinguishing design element that forms a running thread across all the items in a particular collection (the second chapter of this book, 'Devil in the Detail', demonstrates this). This allows for the same last to be used for years, since collections remain available and are not discontinued after a season or two.

Drafting brand new patterns forms the backbone of Trippen's couture approach. Like the sartorial gold standard, Trippen's uppers are conceived of as three-dimensional shapes, running counter to the two-dimensional patterns of conventional shoes, where the inner and outer sides of the upper are almost identical. With just one last, Oehler and Spieth have produced a wide array of designs within any one collection. The subsections under 'Collection' in the second chapter showcase their impressive achievements in pattern development. A truly creative approach to pattern technique is at work, one that sets Trippen apart in the shoe industry. Mars, Fatima and Frog are particularly good examples to illustrate this deviance from traditional pattern technique, since it is immediately apparent that the uppers are cut from patterns unique to each shoe. Yet all are from the Closed collection, based on one and the same last shape.

Luxury is making a real product, and sometimes there are flaws but that's life... instead of covering up with a layer of... something false.

-- Michael Oehler

To Trippen, retaining the same last for multiple designs reduces waste and is faithful to the company's dedication to building a sustainable, socially responsible business. This practice submits to the logic of ecological accountability and also makes economic sense since it cuts down on costs. The fusing of ecological and economic benefits is also illustrated in Trippen's philosophy of simplicity. Only two designers conceptualise, sketch, make up the prototypes, finalise the pattern, cut the upper, and turn out the final sample collection. Prototypes are made in the workshop, and the factory is just 80km north of Berlin, reducing transport to a minimum. Such simplifications in logistics have clear benefits: apart from a smaller carbon footprint, goods are moved quickly, a measure of flexibility is allowed, technical know-how is kept in-house and the shoes remain authentically made in Germany. Such simplicity also extends to Trippen's strategy for advertising and marketing. The designers weighed their choices,

of either increasing the retail price, or go to China and lower production costs, (or) produce our shoes in bigger quantities for economies of scale. But we decided to be simple, clear and direct. When a customer pays for a product, he is paying for it to be made in Europe. We didn't want to sell it at a higher price to accommodate a marketing budget. We wanted a product that always speaks for itself, and what people pay for is no more than what the product is worth.

Just what the product is worth is the aggregate value of the efforts of every part of the shoemaking process taken holistically. Here lies Trippen's greatest asset, its collection, the output of an entire process carried out in-house, from conception and development to production and distribution. Trippen has invested most of its resources in enhancing and adding value to the individual parts of the whole team. Coupled with consideration for the environment, anatomically correct fits and tailor-made designs for different markets and customer requests, a synthesis emerges that is profoundly sustainable, a sustainability that is not just a romantic show of liberal sensibilities, but a lucidly thought-out, necessary process that will support the company's operations in the long run.

HEART
AND
SOLE

___

Naturally – Trippen

Text by Gregor Eisenhauer   Translated by Stella Vitzthum

1980. A young man sets out from Oslo to Bergen on foot, following the railway line. Normally 650 kilometres is the distance people walk in a year. Michael Oehler did it in four weeks. Through the drizzling rain. He had just done sixteen months in a youth psychiatry unit as a conscientious objector to military service. Before that he had dropped out shortly before finishing school. Where he was heading now he was not so sure, but one thing he did know: he had to get away from his home town Lindau, away from Lake Constance, to wider horizons. Four weeks of hiking, of letting his thoughts run free, of tired feet and rubbing lanolin into his shoes every evening. 'It occurred to me then for the first time that shoes are amazing things.' A shoe keeps you down to earth. A shoe is a shoe – is only a shoe if you can walk in it. He stayed six months on a Norwegian farm: shepherding, woodwork, silver jewellery – the whole romantic dropout programme. He could have stayed there, but he wanted what only a city could offer: contact, conflict, change. And he had meanwhile developed a vague idea of what he really wanted.

1980. Stuttgart, Königstrasse: the pedestrian zone of the Swabian capital that will always be provincial however hard it tries. Amused passers-by point at a girl decked out in leather scraps, chains galore, rainbow colours in her hair. A punk! And the shoes! – Pointed, long, weird. Which is just what they were intended to be. A shoe is a shoe – is only a shoe if it causes a stir. Angela Spieth had bought the materials for her outfit from a little old lady in a leather shop that also sold craft supplies and all kinds of remnants. The basics of shoemaking were explained to her, more or less, and the rest had been guesswork, imagination and lots of glue. Her leisure time in Böblingen was spent in the youth centre embroidering jeans, dying textiles, making shoes, painting sunsets, imagining what might happen if the bomb went off and put an end to the boredom of provincial life. One thing she knew for certain: she had to get away, to Hamburg or Berlin or, best of all, to the other end of the world.

School finals and escape at last – to Berlin. But Angela Spieth was no longer punk. Punk was destruction, defiance and Sticky Fingers. The ambitious young lady from a good home had moved on. Angela was now a goth – cool and pale in a new persona that gave her protection as well as some real-life insights into the manipulative effects of fashion.

The whole Berlin thing. Nights in Jungle, the 'in' disco, weekends on the road all over Europe with The Cure and Psychic TV, weekdays studying fashion design at the University of the Arts. But the course had no more than the basics to offer. Her lecturers had never been 'outside' and had no practical experience. A lot of what was taught was too cerebral and academic, while anything in the way of ideas from outside, from the street, was not accepted, let alone welcomed as a creative impulse. Time to move on. London was the next goal, Saint Martins, the fashion and design mecca. But beforehand she had to collect a bit of practical experience.

Michael Oehler had also applied to the University of the Arts – for a place in painting and sculpture. When he was rejected he picked up his portfolio, turned straight around and signed up with a shoemaker. He was going to learn the trade from start to finish, from Heels-While-U-Wait to professional shoe repair to orthopaedic shoemaking. Via extremes to the ideal form. How do you correct unequal leg lengths and disguise deformities? What are the best materials? How can you combine wood, cork and leather? Where do the raw materials come from? How many chemicals are needed to make a shoe soft but durable? Are chemicals needed at all?

For five years, until his master craftsman's examination in 1987, he watched and worked at the side of a master shoemaker from seven in the morning till midday. In the afternoon he set up his own workshop in a back courtyard in Kreuzberg. Custom-made shoes for theatre and film productions or for discerning individual clients. The rules he worked by were firm: an anatomically fitted form, largely non-toxic materials and outstanding craftsmanship of a standard almost unknown in this day and age of mass production. Art is also about ability. Berlin's art colleges recognised this and invited Michael Oehler to speak as guest lecturer for design.

Meanwhile Angela Spieth was far away from Berlin working for Bama, a medium-sized shoe manufacturer in the Odenwald region. An internship in 1987 had turned into a three-year unofficial apprenticeship in production and sales, plus special insights into what is possible in a family business – and what is not. With a young boss, a team of young designers and a new advertising agency she worked on a new collection with lots of mint, lots of pink, garish colours, extravagant lines. The new models were presented at the shoe trade fair in a glass cage. But then, or so it seemed to Angela Spieth, there was a change of course back to conventional designs. Angela Spieth's last day at Bama was her first day with Michael Oehler.

Come together right now – Berlin

Cut to Berlin. The Wall fell, the city seethed. Nightlife went underground – but in what footwear? Militants – left and right – were in army boots, the greens in Birkenstock sandals, with or without socks, the club scene in sneakers where logos counted more than origin, but who cared? What was missing in this city was intelligent footwear.

Angela and Michael met in a design gallery where Bama was exhibiting its new product line. An uncommon encounter in any terms, starting with the visual: weirdo visionary meets goth – a flirt with consequences. They had shoes in common of course, and sunsets, and Lake Constance. And the sense of a new departure. Angela Spieth understood exactly where Michael Oehler was at in his shoemaking, and he could see immediately that she had a perfect eye for design. Sympathy makes synergy. She was keen to see his Berlin workshop, he was grateful for a good price on Bama leather samples. Her last walk through the Bama plant was his first visit to a shoe factory.

But as yet their common ground was not so obvious. Michael Oehler was making one-off shoes in a small Kreuzberg workshop, while Angela Spieth, soon after parting company with Bama, was jetting First Class around the world for the big names in the shoe industry, was invited to Taiwan to inject new life into the domestic shoe scene,

picked up from the airport by a chauffeur-driven car. She slept here in factories, there in five-star hotels, gathering untold experience in the fields of design and production – and one day found herself holding a cheap shoe in her hand, Made in Vietnam, manufacturing cost 99 cents, wage factor negligible. At that moment it became clear to her that she had to escape the fatal logic of the mass market: innovation, imitation, mass production, trash. The same old carousel, a vicious circle of senseless destruction of resources.

By contrast, Michael Oehler's concept of production by hand was high-quality, sparing of material and ecologically sensible, but unthinkable as a model for mass production. Was there no solution? Did it have to be either factory or hand-made? Birkenstock or Prada, ecology or fashion? Falling between stools can be uncomfortable – at the same time it keeps you on the go.

Exile on main street –
Finding a niche and making it habitable

In 1991 Michael Oehler and Angela Spieth visited an old factory in the Harz mountains that in the communist era had made the lasts used in shoe production. There they found old, unused wooden soles from the seventies. Wooden shoes were always manufactured in times of need and after wars: the poor man's boot, the labourer's shoe, ungainly clogs, orthopaedic sandals. Angela Spieth and Michael Oehler saw fashion potential – and a challenge to the craftsman's skill.

They spent four intensive weeks experimenting with the wooden soles in the Kreuzberg workshop, developing their line by trial and error. Their point of departure was and is the anatomy of the foot. Nature is design – it requires no counter-design. The solution: think along nature's lines. No glues. Instead, bond the rubber sole mechanically with the wood. But this made it even narrower than the wood and the result was a twisted ankle, hardly the object of the exercise. The course they were pursuing was clear: from the street to the catwalk, but also back again.

The first trial run produced a dozen gallery shoes. Dyed, nailed and sanded with tender loving care, the rims seared by hand. Not all of them wearable but all innovative in style. The first generation of Trippen shoes. The name? Pinched from the catalogue of an exhibition on historical shoes that happened to be running in Munich. 'Trippen' were wooden undershoes worn in the Middle Ages to protect the then fashionable long-toed poulaines from the filth on the streets.

The exhibition at the Galerie für Kunsthandwerk in Berlin's Pariser Strasse was a huge success. Fashion designers Claudia Skoda and Wolfgang Joop placed orders for their fashion shows. Agents showed interest, and the first pairs appeared in shoe stores. 'They would sell much better if they were cheaper ...' The urgent question now was where to start production.

Don't sell your dreams! From prototype to product

The Trippen principle: Always react immediately when a problem arises. Never sit it out. When obstacles appear there must always be Plan A, B, C, even if that means double the work. Seven days a week, fourteen hours a day if necessary. Anything is possible. And indeed, it was. Students were trained, Serbian draft dodgers with craft skills were recruited from a squat in Berlin-Mitte, and they all came together in Michael Oehler's Kreuzberg workshop on Tempelhofer Berg. One small factory floor within a large disused brewery complex, 70 square meters with a stove heater that also served to make their midday soup. Up to twenty workers squashed into this space together with the machines: Taiwanese working conditions, but with incomparably better morale – and pay. Fifteen marks an hour plus bonuses for extra work on urgent orders. There was no clear dividing line between working nights and partying, The workshop doubled as living space and often as studio too, whenever Angela Spieth returned from her travels for an intensive four-week design stint. The manufactory principle. But where could they get larger quantities of shoes produced? In 1992/3 demand was rising.

'You can come to us!'

In Pirmasens in the German state of Saarland there was a family-owned shoe factory that considered themselves capable of manufacturing Trippen shoes in quantity. But only for the domestic market. They had no confidence in buyers from abroad honouring bills. Angela Spieth and Michael Oehler made the prototypes, agents took orders from boutiques and shoe stores, the factory produced, wanted to produce, the shoes – until emotional upheavals within the family complicated things. Production came to a halt. Michael Oehler led a task force to Pirmasens. Together with one employee and a trainee he took over and restarted production. Angela Spieth, who was still working as freelance designer for other shoe firms, joined the team whenever her regular work allowed. They worked till late into the night for two weeks until the complete collection of wooden shoes was ready for delivery. In the second season the factory produced on schedule but the soles were incorrectly worked and the shoes did not fit. Farewell Pirmasens.

'You can come to us!'

A wealthy Austrian entrepreneur with a very engaging personality was on the lookout for a fashion product for his newly purchased factory near the Czech border. In 1993 he asked Angela Spieth and Michael Oehler to design a new series, not wooden shoes this time but closed leather models. Of course with equal marketing rights. Production was to be in his factory. In Austria his own logo would be used, but internationally the product would be called 'Trippen'. Angela Spieth and Michael Oehler christened the new model of closed leather shoe with a replaceable, patented sole 'Closed'. The entrepreneur liked the design, and he accompanied Spieth and Oehler to London where he introduced the new line to a major importer as 'his' project and Angela Spieth and Michael Oehler as 'his' designers. Farewell Austria.

'You can come to us!'

September 1994, GDS international shoe fair - The Trippen stand: all of 12 square meters and even this only thanks to a favour from a friend in the shoe business. A dozen models, five 'Closed' and seven wooden shoes. Two cobbler's stools for Angela Spieth and Michael Oehler, the stand itself done out in white florists' paper, on the walls rough boards at eye level. One shoe per board. Minimal Art. The response? The big names – Teva, Airwalk, Reef Brazil, Simple – were standing in line, outbidding each other to buy the collection. 150,000 dollars. Come on, shake on it! Don't sell your dreams! Angela Spieth and Michael Oehler thought, 'If they offer us so much money our collection must be damned good. In which case we'll simply make it ourselves.' Production, marketing and sales.

Trippen A. Spieth, M. Oehler GmbH was founded on 22 December 1994. Christmas had come early that year.

One last time: 'You can come to us!'

The international buzz around the Trippen stand did not go unnoticed by the young Italian across the aisle. 'Where do you produce? Come to us, to Italy!' In his father's day the factory had employed three hundred people. His father had meanwhile retired from the day-to-day running of the business and now there were only forty-five employees. When they were subsequently faced with producing the unusually work-intensive Trippen models parallel to an order for a major client it proved far too much for them. The task force sprang into action once again. Michael Oehler drove to Padua with five employees, occupied the factory and supervised every step of production, lending a hand himself when necessary. The second and final sole seam. There was no machine to do the job. It would have to be glued. 'No way!' ruled Angela Spieth. Either two seams or nothing. Anything less was not a Trippen shoe. SOS to all factories in the area.

A firm in Friuli was prepared to finish the job. The Veronese company that had found them now provided the transport. The half-finished shoes, lasts and leather punches were all loaded. Suddenly the factory patriarch placed himself in front of the lorry and demanded the payment agreed on for finished production. Without deductions. 'The whole amount, or no freight papers!' They didn't have the money to hand, and he hadn't earned it anyway. What could they do? The truck driver was getting impatient. 'Scusi, either we go or I'll have to unload.' Unloading would have meant bankruptcy. A business start-up loan had been approved by a Berlin bank but the money was not yet in their account. Where could they get the cash? One last try – Michael Oehler rang his mother, who he had not spoken to for some time. She sent the money by SWIFT transfer. Forty thousand deutschmarks from bank to bank within an hour, and thirty minutes later the truck set off for Friuli with the half-finished shoes.

A cold factory building, one old man, hardly any machines. These still had to be collected from houses around the area. Over the next three weeks Trippen shoes were produced from seven in the morning until midnight. They were four weeks behind delivery date, but still in time: their customers accepted the goods. The happy ending was still to come. The Italian lira devalued, thus more or less offsetting the excessive payment that had been extorted from them, and the little factory in Friuli proved to be a lucky strike. From then on it was Trippen's production centre in Italy.

I can't wait to meet you – 'We'll come to you!'

Paris, Spring 1995 'Workshop' fashion fair. This time there was no producer, no agent queuing at their stand. Not a single sale in seven days. Then, on the last day, the shoestore in Paris placed an order. For two seasons they displayed Trippen shoes. And what gets into this Paris shop window is what anybody who is anybody in avant-garde fashion wants to have: Yohji Yamamoto, Barbara Bui, Perry Ellis. Trippen had made it into the top league of international designers.

Agents and fashion-makers from Japan in particular were interested in this exotic duo from Germany. Trippen exports to Japan barely reached six hundred pairs in 1996 but that was enough to put at least one pair into every major shoestore in Tokyo and Osaka. Trippen was big in Japan.

The president of a Japanese trading firm, one of the first to be smitten by the Trippen aesthetic after discovering the shoes in a Paris shop and wearing them himself, approached Angela Spieth and Michael Oehler with a proposal to be their sole distributor in Japan. They flew to Tokyo to inspect possible locations. He himself then came to Berlin in 1997 where negotiations were concluded swiftly and easily. 'Whatever you want …' The answer was instant: 'We want ten shops in Japan!'

In Germany Trippen had already opened its first shop in summer 1995 in Hackesche Höfe, a trendy courtyard complex in the centre of Berlin. In the first one and a half years every pair of shoes was sold by Angela Spieth or Michael Oehler personally. The shop doubled as office, with a provisional storeroom located above the toilet.

When Christo's Wrapped Reichstag brought a flood of tourists to the city, they sold shoes night and day. When the Hackesche Höfe complex underwent a total renovation, customers rarely even found the shop. But otherwise the ups and downs of the economy and the dictates of fashion have not affected the Trippen shops. The concept is simple: the shop has to supply the right setting for the shoe. That's all.

On the floor, terracotta tiles feature reliefs of their first wooden shoes. On the walls, plain white showcases display single pairs of shoes. Throughout the shop, low platforms present the collection from another angle. Antique African stools, vaguely reminiscent of the traditional cobbler's stool, also communicate endurance as opposed to seasonal transience. No price or size tags, instead friendly staff attentive to the customer's needs.

Japan's first Trippen shop opened in Tokyo in September 1997, planned and supervised down to the last detail by Angela Spieth. Interior details as in the Berlin store: terracotta tiles, wall display, subtle lighting. Even a duplicate of the 'throne', where a client traditionally sat for a fitting at the custom shoemaker's, was freighted to Tokyo. The idea proved superfluous and it was never used. A Japanese customer does not take a high seat, let alone a throne. In other respects customer mentality and taste in Japan were no different from Europe. Ten shops opened one after another. Dreams come true. And even though a few of them have had to close as a result of the economic crisis in Japan, Taiwan had been watching closely

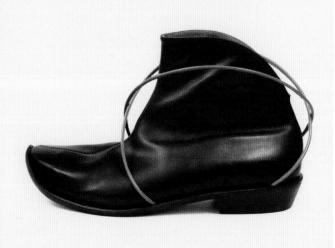

erste BERLINER SCHUH

vom
7.9
bis
11.10.91 Dienstag bis Freitag
12.00 bis 18.00 Uhr
Samstag 10.00 bis 13.00 Uhr

Pariserstrasse 12
1000 Berlin 15
U9 - Spichernstrasse

and the door to the entire Asian market opened, with the result that to this day it accounts for a large part of Trippen's turnover. New European markets developed too. In Belgium and France famous fashion labels ordered Trippen shoes as special accessories to their collections.

The only thing they needed now to be totally hip was a shop in London! 1999, Covent Garden, the ultimate shopping location. Two shops were available. High rent with a large window, or low rent with a small window? Modesty does not always pay.

A 7.5-tonne lorry and trailer were loaded with everything needed for setting up the new shop. Followed by a convoy of buses for the staff, they crossed the Channel and laboured night and day for two weeks setting up the new store in Trippen style. A cut took Michael Oehler on an odyssey through three hospitals before the bleeding was stopped, giving him unexpected insights into the idiosyncrasies of the British health service and a premonition that London might not be his lucky star.

After one year the rent tripled, but the small shop window was hardly noticed by passers-by. The London adventure lasted two years altogether. It was not a success, but not a complete failure either. While the crowds of customers they had hoped for did not appear, trend scouts did, and they made Trippen popular in the Crown Colony of Hong Kong.

How high the moon –
From workshop to a factory of their own

Trippen expanded steadily after the Paris fair in spring 1995. Professionalisation, even though not always welcomed by either the employees or the duo at the helm, took place at all levels. Michael Oehler capitulated at last and acquired a driving licence. It was simply no longer feasible to transport ten boxes of insoles by train to Italy, manhandling them singly, one after another, from platform to carriage.

In 1996 their first real office opened in Chausseestrasse, Berlin-Mitte, a former fitness studio in a condemned building. The heating did not work but the elevator did, just as long as you kept your finger on the button. Keep pushing. Now they even had a conference room, scene of many briefings for the initial staff of nine – and of many job interviews.

Facing page, clockwise from top left

First, second and fourth Oehler's handmade designs before founding Trippen.

Third Erste Berliner Schuhausstellung (first Berlin shoe exhibition) at the Galerie Kunsthandwerk Berlin, 1991.

Fifth Wooden shoe collection, spring/summer 1993.

At first these were conducted in laid-back Kreuzberg style. 'What do you feel like doing? Where do you think your strengths lie?' The job description then evolved from there. Back then it was personal chemistry, not qualifications and references that counted – understandably, since most were students or came from other fields and had no shoemaking skills. Over the years things have become more professional here too. Applicants are now invited to four interviews. Angela Spieth explains what Trippen expects of them in the workplace. Michael Oehler listens to what they expect from Trippen and works out how they can combine their respective ambitions most effectively. The bookkeeping and sales staff check their qualifications and personal skills.

Good employees are not easy to find. Trippen are still looking for a No. 3 to ease the admin load at the top. Meanwhile, several unsuccessful attempts later, the main thing is to find someone to help at any level.

Only in apprentice recruitment has nothing changed over the years. There the old rule still holds: apprentices are hired by apprentices.

As pressure on production increased with the Trippen boom in Japan and elsewhere, it became clear that the family business in Friuli could not keep up with demand. The workshop model was stretched to its limits, especially where jealously guarded family interests precluded involving other, urgently needed – even closely related – producers. In 1996 things came to a head. A new production location had to be found.

From an earlier visit to Portugal Angela Spieth knew of a shoe factory in São João de Madeira that she believed could produce Trippen shoes. One telephone call and they were on their way. With a busload of tools and materials the pair drove from Berlin via Italy to Portugal and then back to Berlin for fresh supplies. Five thousand kilometres. All in all, Angela has driven one million kilometres to date, the late-starter Michael seven hundred thousand.

Production got off to a good start in the test phase: one thousand pairs. Now for the real thing. Soles, leather and everything else was driven down. Michael Oehler even slept in the car to guard the leather and avoid risks at all costs. But a nasty surprise was waiting for them. Quality dropped and the work was careless: an understanding for the standards required was clearly lacking. Everything was slightly askew, less than perfect, simply not good enough to pack. Angela Spieth spent night after night sorting out substandard shoes and pairing the remaining ones anew. The piles of rejects grew higher and higher.

The decision was made. Back to Italy, where the family problems had finally been resolved – riunificazione! – and production could expand to a sustainable long-term level.

In 1997 an important and long overdue step was also taken in Berlin. The workshop on Tempelhofer Berg where Michael Oehler had worked for ten years was closed. The party was over. Friends become employees. A poignant moment for Michael Oehler: 'I'm no longer a shoemaker – I am now a businessman.' The master craftsman who had treated every member of the team as an apprentice, who had tested every step with them and prepared the next day's material for each of them, had become a manager.

An unrenovated factory floor in Gerichtstrasse provided an interim solution. The different production stages were now separated spatially. Designing, cutting, sanding, sewing, finishing. Three apprentices worked here alongside twenty or so students, some of whom had difficulty adapting to the new conditions of more or less industrial production. The working environment was still permeated by the old Kreuzberg spirit – not least as a result of the missing lavatory door – but the special aura of the one big communal workroom was gone. It made no difference that Michael Oehler made a point of swinging into action again himself to renovate the kitchen. The concrete casings collapsed, the walls bulged, the storage problems remained unresolved. It was more evident than ever that he had to delegate.

A moment to myself – 'We're leaving the firm!'

By the end of 2000 Trippen had sold sixty thousand shoes and was in the black for the first time. After replacing company vehicles there was a distribution of profits to employees. There were ulterior motives for this. In the summer a workshop was organised in a small seaside hotel in Italy for everyone in the firm. Also present was a business consultant and psychologist who presented a company ownership model to the Trippen employees.

The management duo wanted a twelve-month break to regenerate. In the long term, the idea was that the employees would take over the firm. But group dynamics obey laws of their own. Suddenly Angela Spieth and Michael Oehler found themselves subjected to detailed criticism of their style of management. The issue of employee ownership was not even dealt with. The shareholder model had failed: one side was not prepared to take risks, the other side had been too hasty.

Nonetheless Angela Spieth and Michael Oehler both took time out, withdrawing from the office, but naturally not from the creative and production side of things, from January to October 2001. Then came the emergency call: either come back or everything collapses. The immediate result of this experience was the purchase of a computer system to take care of the logistics – without staff assistance if need be.

Meanwhile the firm had expanded to eighty-five employees. 2002 saw not only the opening of two new shops in Berlin but also the founding of 'Trippen direkt', a company within the company devoted exclusively to running the shops and internet sales. The aim was to achieve more independence from third parties, including the

agents who until then had represented Trippen in Germany and abroad. Not all of the separations that followed were as amicable as in Italy three years earlier.

In 1999 a famous agent for the Italian market offered to sell Trippen shoes, a proposal Angela Spieth and Michael Oehler happily agreed to. When it turned out after the first season that Trippen was selling very well in Italy, but not in the shops the agent had been supplying, they asked him to come and see them. The question was whether to continue working together. 'Shall we toss?' The agent was either too amazed or too proud to refuse. He lost the toss and that was that. 'An unusual way of deciding things? Not for us. When arguments seem equally strong on both sides, we toss. It's worked fine so far!'

Xplore, xpand, xperience – Trippen in the saturation phase

New Year 2001 saw Trippen installed in a new and spacious office in Kiefholzstrasse. New Economy style, loft atmosphere, a breathtaking view over Berlin. In this setting even occasional chaos looks decorative. Angela Spieth and Michael Oehler still share a studio, but the installation of a dividing wall with sound-proof door is imminent. At last, after years of having no choice, they now admit to having quite different tastes in music.

On the production side the most significant milestone has been the end of the Kreuzberg model. In 1998 their new workshop opened in Zehdenick, a small town not far from Berlin. Here a large East German shoe factory had closed down after reunification. The idea now, starting in a small way, was to establish a German factory with professionally skilled workers, the first of whom were between fifty and sixty years of age. They had to make do with a dilapidated wooden shack until a new building was purchased in 2004, formerly the posh canteen of a computer factory. Workshop finally becomes factory. With this factory in mind, the new Penna collection, featuring an innovative sole, was designed and made ready for production that same year.

Strategic errors are often evident only when catastrophe has already struck. Trippen has only one producer for the soles. Production is in full swing. A sole with a strange white discharge is noticed. Then another. All the cartons are unpacked, all the shoes examined. Every sole is sweating a white silicate. The shoes are unwearable. The producer refuses to believe them and in fact the soles do leave his factory without any noticeable defects. It is only during transport that the problem appears. The cause? To satisfy German environmental regulations a chemical has been substituted – with near-catastrophic results. The Trippen philosophy 'Don't sit it out – react immediately' was put to its hardest test to date. A desperate search for an antidote began. Silicon! Temporary staff were engaged and set to work. The sole of every single shoe had to be heated with a hairdryer, rubbed with silicon, wiped and repacked. Twenty thousand pairs of shoes.

The hard thing about success is that it has to be proved again and again.

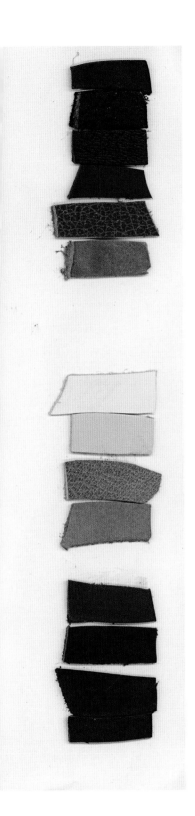

It's the song not the singer – What counts ... the idea

Success is a question of statistics. Nearly one hundred twenty thousand shoes sold and a turnover of 10 million euros in 2009. Nine hundred and fifty models, eight hundred and fifty of these available any time. More than one hundred and fifty employees. Trippen shoes sold in thirty-five countries around the world. Four hundred and fifty associated stores globally, one hundred and fifty of them in Germany. Two patents and more than a dozen designs and patterns registered. And – the downside of success – Trippen shoes are being copied all over the world.

Success equals profit. But profit is not the focus of the business – and yet it is the focus insofar as it guarantees Trippen's continued existence. Its employees depend on a six figure sum being paid out in wages each month. Trippen is nevertheless not first and foremost about business. It is an entrepreneurial idea that has to prove itself economically again and again.

This demands a lot from employees, sometimes too much where many have come from other backgrounds. A business is a family is a business that sometimes has to support people going through a rough time. 'We don't do anything special ... just the normal human thing' – which in a quietly revolutionary way has transformed the old economic model of family business as workshop into workshop as family business and ultimately into the futuristic concept of a business cooperative with owner liability.

Liability above all in the creative sense. The work partnership between Angela Spieth and Michael Oehler is a guarantee for dynamic product development. The collection designer and the number cruncher, the trend scout and the quality fanatic are an indivisible team. Many are the contracts they have formally drawn up and never signed, many the power struggles doggedly contested. In the early days they were permanently at loggerheads. They have had to work hard for the negotiating skills they now possess.

But Trippen is more than the now quarrelsome, now harmonious interplay between two protagonists united against the rest of the business world. Traces of the punk and the weirdo visionary are still lurking there, firing their determination to prove to all the doubters that the good and beautiful and ecologically sound shoe is possible. They have proved it: it is possible.

Success is: sowing ideas that it is impossible to imagine life without. A shoe is a shoe – is a statement of art.

Part of Trippen's archives

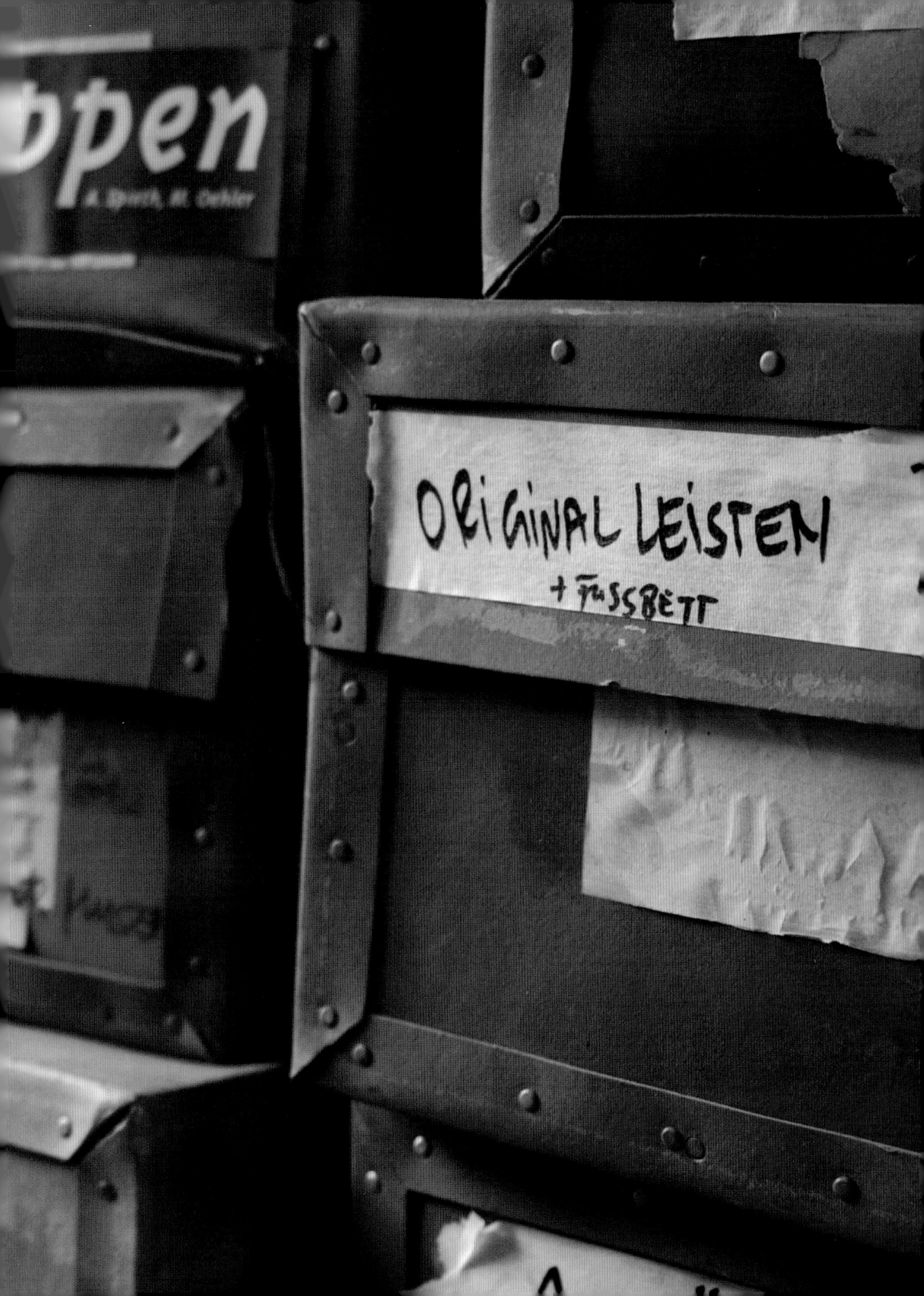
ORIGINAL LEISTEN
+ FUSSBETT

DEVIL IN THE DETAIL

Discovering the birth of an idea in the landscape of an artist's mind is a curious encounter. What visions conjured, what muse obeyed, what fantasies indulged determine the final work of art in myriad ways. For Trippen, sometimes the names give the game away. Loose strips of leather cascade over the instep on a sandal named Niagara; Mountains, Shark, Fire and Flames boast dramatically jagged edges; Cactus has triangular incisions; the beauty of Palace lies in its profile, where the silhouette of Oriental pagoda eaves is beheld.

Sometimes the names sound like Dickensian characters – Parzival. Orinoco. Mustafa. Moskau. Jubilee. Taking on lives of their own, they display personalities that emerge from particular combinations of material and technique. These can be as complex and ingenious as uppers featuring leather slits, washing and tie-dying goatskin, or having Japanese calligraphy cut into box-like rubber soles. However, they may also be as simple as a strong graphic silhouette, overlapping pieces of leather on the upper, or an evocative line or curve.

The mind-boggling range of designs (literally close to a thousand of them) was inspired by fields as varied as sport (Kendo, Wrestler), architecture (Coco, Cathedral, Fatima), literature (Poe, Widow, Kafka), dance (Swan, Waltz, Tango), eroticism (Bondage, Fetish) religion (Bishop, Nun, Priest) and transport (Boat, Car, Train, Visions). In the midst of this sweeping scope of categories, two recurring motifs stand out – Greco-Roman culture and the Middle Ages, particularly medieval warfare. As they have for other fields, both artistic and scientific, these two motifs have provided rich fodder for Trippen's designers. A cursory glance at Trippen's list of shoe models surfaced Aphrodite, with open lacing; Isis, with elk leather twirls climbing up the ankle; and Troja, a lace-up boot. More inspiration from antiquity led to the creation of Hera, Skylla, Poseidon and Aurora. Significantly, four amongst the dozen all-time Trippen bestsellers are Zeus, Helena, Sparta and Warrior. These designs feature iconic Hellenic elements such as laces and wrapped leather pieces, elements that have proven themselves perennial design favourites.

The medieval world provided inspiration for many designs, particularly in Trippen's range of boots and booties. Lear, Templar, Knight and Crusader are almost primitive-looking boots complete with overlapping flaps and buckled straps while the lines of Dome, a bootie, echo medieval religious architecture. Dante references a type of medieval shoes known as Bärentatzen, or bear paws, while Parzival recalls the leather clothing of medieval knights. The rustic character of these styles is deliberately honed, for it directly articulates the sober, austere aesthetic of a Trippen shoe.

This, perhaps, might be the most important thing of all to bear in mind. In the end, the shoes speak for themselves. Stripping away their names, their similitude to their real-life counterparts and the inspiration that spawned their design, the shoes are located at the intersections between imagination, art, functionality and construction.

This chapter has been structured to respect each design for what it is, rather than what it stands for or looks like. Starting with a list of ten of Trippen's all-time bestselling designs which have become modern classics, the chapter then goes back in time to 1992 with 'Before Trippen'. This section features designs made from wood for Erste Berliner Schuhausstellung (first Berlin shoe exhibition), organised by Michael Oehler at the Galerie für Kunsthandwerk, Berlin, as well as Recycled, a collection made from old jeans, carpets and motorcycle tyres. In limited runs and mostly no longer in production, these designs are significant in charting the evolution of Trippen, instrumental as they are in the formation of the brand's philosophy regarding craft, technique and the sustainable use of material.

The section after is organised chronologically, showcasing the standouts of each year's production. Whether by a feat of construction, an avant-garde sole design, an innovative cut or experimentally new type of leather, the featured shoes of each year are marvels of design or technique, often both. Rather than simply being a catalogue of Trippen shoes, this section flaunts the continuous originality of the designers, who have dared to dream up something truly different and creative, year after year.

'Collection' is organised differently. The ten sub-sections comprise designs that were conceptualised as part of a larger whole, with each whole having unique attributes. While collections such as Boots and Closed are wider in range and encompass several types of material and technique, others such as Penna, Cup, x + o and more recently, Box and Happy have distinct features, in particular, distinct soles.

The final part of the chapter is classified thematically. Instead of a collection conceived within a particular family with a signature sole, the shoes in 'Theme' have been grouped on hindsight. Assessing Trippen's output through the years, Angela Spieth identified eight themes, based on material, silhouette, function, or design, that predominated. She then handpicked individual designs she identified as consistent with these themes – slits, elk, pleats, knots, protection, graphics, overlaps and fur. The result is an unusual look at the brand through the eyes of one of its founders, who is today still principally in charge of design for the house. Deviating from a chronology, 'Theme' reveals to the consumer that it is in the one-of-its-kind details that Trippen excels in. And if that is where the devil lurks, the people at Trippen are more than happy to be his advocate in the business of shoe manufacturing.

Templar

Knight

Fatima

Cutting knives

ALL TIME BESTSELLERS

Bomb

Haferl

Service

Zeus

Hysterie

Zen

Helena

Sparta

Mug

Travel

Golf

Warrior

Store display for Trippen Gallery store in Berlin

PRODUCTS

Before Trippen

Year 1993 – 2009

Collections

Themes

Before Trippen

Knappe

Juwel

Karat

Recycled

The desire to generate less waste with a
brand-new product led to the creation of
the Recycled collection. Motorbike tyres
were used for the soles, carpet remnants for
the footbed, denim and cord fabrics for the
uppers and bicycle tubes as elastics.

Schnecke

Assi

Prototypes Wood

Making their debuts at the Galerie für
Kunsthandwerk in 1992 to great acclaim,
these very early handmade wooden prototypes
are the precursors to the ongoing collection
of wooden clogs. They are also the brand's
namesake: in medieval times trippen were
wooden soles strapped to shoes to protect the
latter from the dirt on unpaved streets.

Year 1993 – 2009

Strahl

1993

Wooden clogs remain close to the beating
heart of Trippen, and Strahl is one of the
pioneers in the company's history, making
its debut at a Berlin art gallery in 1992.
Crafted from virgin wood, these wood
sculptures are combined with thick natural
leather and demonstrate what Trippen excels
in: the marriage of traditional handicraft
with industrial expertise.

Yen

1995

Another pioneer, Yen, comes from Closed, the
collection introduced in 1994 and an enduring
bestseller ever since. The collection's patented
rubber sole and pre-moulded cork insole
provide flexibility and shock absorption;
uppers are sewn twice to the removable sole
that is exchangeable, ensuring comfort for the
wearer and longevity for the shoe.

Spock

1996

Spock is from the Sheepskin Closed
collection, comprising modern interpretations
of traditional sheepskin boots. These were
inspired by the bitterly cold winter of 1995.

Gas

Rohr

1997

While the architecture of bridges were the inspiration behind the 1997 spring/summer collection, rubber tubes were an unusual choice of material for the strappy clogs. The bold standout gas tubing in Gas and Rohr are two particularly vivid examples, with more than a hint of the punk influences that characterised Angela Spieth's youth.

Bonny

Claudia

1998

top   The introduction of felt, an important European traditional shoe material, was inspired by uniforms and resulted in winter shoes that are both flexible and built to last.

middle   Interchangeable pairs of wedge heels, a low heel for daywear and a high heel for evening wear are fixed to the rubber soles of Claudia using a peg-and-hole joint, making the change from day to night effortless.

bottom   The Goodyear shoe is the eponymous design crafted using the construction technique traditionally used for mountain boots. The Trippen version boasts a sturdy, waterproof sole with arch suppport and a robust stitch.

Goodyear-Low

Bone

Dandy

1999

top Bone is a one-size-fits-all model that can be adjusted to the wearer's foot with a metal screw between the ball of the foot and the heel of the wooden sole. Like Claudia and Carola in the Cham collection, Bone also has exchangeable heels: high or flat.

bottom Elk leather lends its remarkable softness and elasticity to the ongoing Elk collection, which proves that a shoe can indeed be as much a pleasure to wear as a well-loved sweater. 1999 marks the introduction of this material to the Trippen family.

Stripe

2000

Summer 2000 saw the introduction of
innovative self-forming footbeds made of felt
used in the debut leather sandal collection.
Layers of felt make up the footbed that
moulds to the wearer's foot according to an
individual's weight distribution. This offers
maximum comfort and customised support,
together with the safety belt-like straps
keeping the foot in place.

Mug

2001

The desire to create an ergonomic shoe
that simulated the feeling of walking in
socks resulted in the Cup collection. The
resulting footbed holds and cups the foot,
simultaneously forming the skeleton of the
shoe. Some designs from Cup eventually
formed part of the Trippen for Issey Miyake
label, handpicked by the famous Japanese
design house.

Falte

2002

Clearly a part of the Graphic Closed
collection featuring daring experiments
in contour and silhouette, Falte plays with
the contrast between the organic form of
the last and the geometric cut of the upper.
The quarter is extended and, from the side,
looks like a square. The line of stitching
underscores this impression optically.

Mexico

2003

The Closed collection of boots boasts many of Trippen's bestsellers. Luxurious yet functional, the boots are designed to be lifelong favourites. Mexico is a knee-high boot that can be tied around the leg in any desired fashion that fits almost everyone.

Amira

2004

The Penna collection is based on the
principles of a Moccasin-type construction;
soft leather uppers are sewn onto a flexible
sole unit, eliminating the need for solvent-
based adhesives. The sole, with its concave
shape, offers maximum shock absorption,
while the shoe itself works without a
footbed, allowing the foot to shape its own
anatomically formed insole.

Dyed

2005

The Lavato ('washed' in Italian) collection
is another Trippen innovation, featuring
denim-lined sheep or goatskin material
that is washed at high temperatures and
subsequently dyed by hand. Thanks to the
tie-dye effect with its uneven colouring, as
seen here in Dyed, the result of this elaborate
process is a unique look for every shoe.

A4 Bag

2006

The leather for the bags come from the same
tannery as the leather for Trippen's shoes and
is also vegetable-tanned. The same design is
offered in three sizes: small (A5), large (A4)
and XXL (A3). A patented strap along the
front keeps belongings safe from theft.

Service

2007

2007 was the year the x+os collection won the iF Product Design Award as well as the German Shoe and Leather Goods Prize. In 2008, the same collection was nominated for the Design Award of the Federal Republic of Germany. Credit goes to the innovative cross-shaped wedge sole which reduces the shoe's weight and provides lateral stability. The uppers are sewn to the sole, with the shape provided by seams, doing away with solvent-based adhesives and making recycling easy.

Yacht

2008

Joining the ranks of the smooth summer
sole and the more textured winter sole of
the Cup collection, is another new Trippen
innovation, the crepe sole, also made from
100% rubber. This Crepe collection features
layers of high-quality rubber and addresses
the increasingly important need for socially
responsible materials.

Boss

Soul

2009

top Inspired by basketball high tops, the Box collection is set to be a new Trippen classic. Already iconic in appearance with two cuboids on the sole which facilitate a rolling motion, the collection's the rubber sole and embedded air chambers provide optimum shock absorption. The seam between the sole and the shaft can be unravelled so that old soles can be removed, recycled and replaced.

bottom The Happy collection boasts good looks, comfort and function with its platform sole and eight-centimetre heel. It is also intelligently built: extra reinforcements within the heel and a specially designed inflexible insole stabilises the sole unit, while elaborately positioned air chambers in the sole guarantee excellent shock absorption.

Soles for the Cup collection

Collections

Boots

Knight

Warrior

Medea

Hysterie

Eskimo

Bubble

Miami

Leguan

Long

Santa Fe

Tower

Nordic

Mexico

Reptile

Nox

Priest

Waran

Overknee

Twiggy

Thule

Templar

Collections
Box

Bold

Memphis

Emotion

Boss

Rand

Channel

Ringer

Tube

Noon

Rim

Collections
Closed

Frame

Graphic   Burst

Haferl

Baden-Württemberg International Design-Award 1996/1997

Liv

Sheet

Tyler

Scooter

Stitch

X-Stitch

Sparta

Helena

Fold

Eaton

Ascot (black)

Ascot (brown)

Prison

Liebchen

Stan (brown)   Stan (black)

Loipe

Parzival

Fun (khaki)

Fun (black)

Bogen

Girly

Mascha

Vivienne (plum)

Vivienne (olive)

Vivienne (black)

Kongo

Loafer

Lulu

Mountains

Nomad

Vision

Core

Bauer

Kraft

Chelsea Black

Omen

Crisp

Crystal

Pina

Gangster

Scorpion

Whale

Scar

Boom

Will

Page

Worms (white)

Wave

Worms (black)

Collections

Cup

Bowl

Good Design Award USA 2001
Good Design Award Japan 2001
Red Dot Award 2001

Cream (mauve)

Cream (black)

Thriller

Pull

Floral (mauve)

Floral (black)

Africa Olive

Isis Black

Button

Tiba

Plate

Short

King (white)

King (black)

Polo (white)

Polo (black)

Cute (white multi)

Charm (orange)

Cute (black multi)

Charm (yellow)

Cute (black)

Charm (black)

Kind

Sunday

Lyric

Lucky

Till

Muse

Mug

Snob

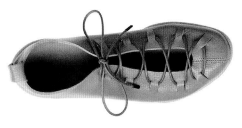

Knife

Surf

Police

Waltz

Wrestler

Sleek (black)

Sleek (lilac)

Scotch (black)

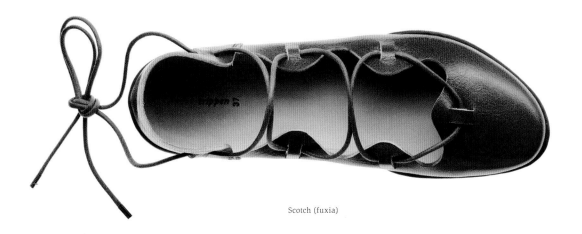

Scotch (fuxia)

Collections

Happy

Blues

Spirit

Soul

Collections

Kids

The most colour-drenched collection in Trippen's range of designs, the children's collection features uppers that mimic the fit and feel of a sock with no middle soles or insoles. They also have thoughtfully selected soft crepe outer soles, especially suited for children's feet.

Mesh

Dance

Hussar

Nadja

Snow

Camus (pink)

Camus (yellow)

Coil

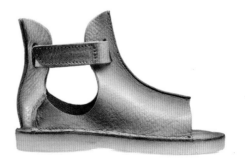

Neptun

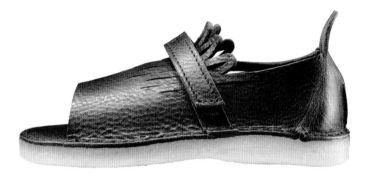

Motion

Sandal

Liebchen

Fold (olive)

Fold (khaki)

Dragon (red)

Dragon (petrol)

Round

Calimero

Knife

Harriet

Made

Zopf

Sid (olive)

Sid (aqua)

View (yellow)

View (kobalt)

Collections

Penna

Good Design Award USA 2004
The Design Award of the Federal Republic of Germany Nominee 2006

Annette

Mehmet

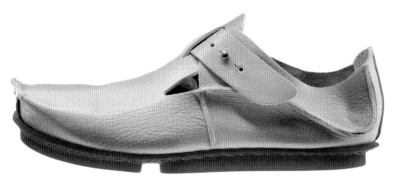

Kalif

Ideal (cloud)

Ideal (black)

Dance (black)

Dance (mauve)

Match (black)

Match (stellar)

Country

Taurus

Malika

Thomas

Rubens (black)

Rubens (granit)

Travel (beige)

Travel (black)

Made (lilac)

Made (black)

Straight

Zopf

Round

Plain

Kajak

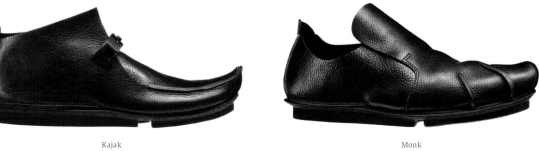

Monk

Tribe

Mystic

Circe

Enigma

Leyla

Bloc

Gothic

Herz

Lou

Road

Schnecke

Kuh

Dust

Canoe

Great

Knit (silver)

Knit (black)

Curls (cuoio)

Curls (black)

Flood

Aphrodite

Faustina

Nixe

Coil

Neptun

Nymphe (black)

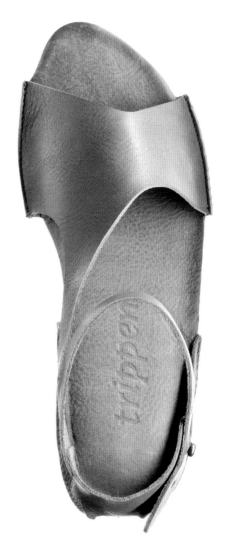

Nymphe (cloud)

Collections

Wooden Clogs

Paris

P1

Hilton

Rohr

Gas

Strahl

Bad

Zulu

Coco

Welle

Slingshot

Mies

Ritzy

Orinoco

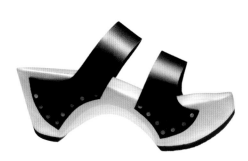

Nuba

Yin

Sling

Mogami

Tango

Moskau

Pony

Ibis

Hopper

Domina

Zorro

Butch

Ron

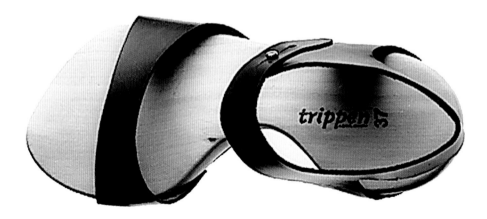

Joy

George

Neck

Kokone

Puck

Hutu

Zen

Callas

Collections

x + o

Service

iF product design award 2007
German Shoe and Leather Goods Prize 2007
The Design Award of the Federal Republic of Germany Nominee 2008

Amaze

End

Clear (mauve)

Clear (stellar)

Exotic

Ocean

Stream

Style

Limit (perla)

Play

Limit (black)

Choral (granit)

Choral (black)

40s (black)

40s (flesh)

Walhalla (black)

Walhalla (red)

Holy

60s

Zaun

Skylla

Kilt

Gaia (black)

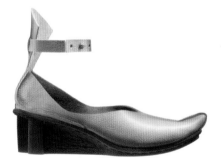

Gaia (cloud)

Tidy (wine)

Tidy (black)

Edel

Stil

Aurora

Dome

Sun

Trail

Vogue-Hi

Vogue

Shoeboxes ready and waiting

Nailing wooden shoes individually by hand

Themes

Elk

Ballett

Beutel

Bond

Chaos

Copy

Hudson

Easy (perla)

Eccentric

Easy (black)

Oper

Pluto (black)

Pluto (coral)

Mars (black)

Mars (pink)

Pausch (black)

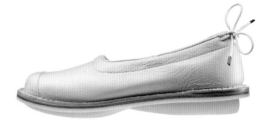

Pausch (rose)

Ingrid

Knot

Sack

Themes

Fur

Fury

Beast

Yak

x2

Turn

Orb

Kante

Best

Cinema

Rectangle

Dragon

Shanghai

Bomb

Boat

Kafka

Shark

Ship

Themes

Graphics

Arguably the most visually striking and
technically challenging amongst all of
Trippen's products, the shoes under the
loose thematic grouping of Graphics flaunt
Trippen's unique, sustainable approach to
cutting patterns for uppers. Every Trippen
shoe is based on a single last with its
own pattern drafted completely anew,
contrary to the widespread practice of
having new lasts for every collection while
only slightly modifying the basic patterns.
This foldout section showcases some
stunningly innovative examples. Fatima's
spiral-shaped top line echoes the interior
of The Guggenheim. Parachute's creases
that fall around the calf are inspired by
parachutes and Chinese lanterns. Bomb,
an all-time bestseller, is cut to fit like a
cosy slipper; while Lotus is one of Spieth's
favourite designs for its experimentation
with extremities.

Mondrian

Tulpe

Palace

131

Inside Out

Parachute

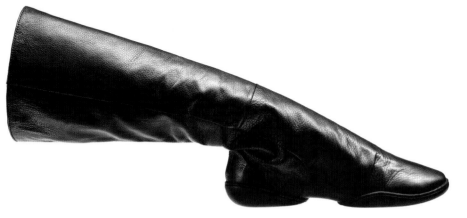

Lotus

Elfe (fuxia)

Elfe (black)

Falte

Fatima

Fire

Rhino

Themes

Knots

Isis (black)

China (black)

China (coral)

Isis (flieder)

Swirl

Bound

Göttin

Love

Januar

Goddess

Glory

Tie

Octopus

Float

Como

Tornado

Elegance

Widow

Themes

Overlaps

Horse

Fly   Pilot

Devil (female)

Devil (male)

Charly

Roof

Car

Speed

Wappen (mud)

Wappen (black)

Tent

Loose

Themes

Pleats

Pleats (cuoio)

Pleats (black)

Pleats (granit)

Nox

Shrink

Arctic

Lena (black)

Lena (steel)

Crash (olive)

Crash (black)

Jetset (black)

Jetset (steel)

Rose (white)

Rose (black)

Lily   Pretty

Swan

Scarf

Cape

Crush

Themes

Protection

Jack

Bob

Dale

Zeus

Switch

Band (espresso)

Band (black)

Themes

Slits

Hi-Cut / Sword

Award Design Center Stuttgart 1999
I.D. Annual Design Award 2000
Good Design Award USA 2000

Trippen's winter 2000 collection centred on the theme of protection, and the resultant designs were based on combining the uses of hard and soft leathers. The multiple award-winning Hi-Cut/Sword possesses a close-fitting soft inner boot with a hard protective outer shell of vegetable-tanned calf leather. In terms of construction technique, Hi-Cut/Sword was an achievement in boot making. Because of their long shafts, conventional boots are typically made of blocked leather or fashioned with a middle seam. For Hi-Cut/Sword, the curve is achieved with horizontal incisions in the leather, combining inventiveness with artistry, serving design with technique. The design was later re-launched as Hi-Cut, with narrower incisions.

Kaviar (khaki)

Kaviar (black)

El

Mesh (black)

Mesh (granit)

Spencer

Jail

Bird

Hutch

Fish (black)

Fish (lilac)

Cage (brown)

Cage (black)

Sport (male)

Sport (female)

Slash

Voodoo

Jubilee (flesh)

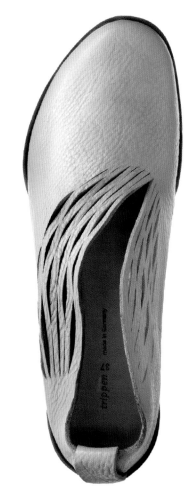

Move (cloud)

Jubilee (black)

Move (black)

Catch

Glow

Dante

Rembrandt

Lo-Cut

Bogen

Fence

Ray

Open

Motion

Bloom

Basta

Cactus (black)

Cactus (cloud)

Spider (black)

Spider (white)

Perm

Chop

Clod

Stretch

A shelf of sample designs

THROUGH THE LOOKING GLASS

The story of Trippen's inception is somewhat legendary. In 1991 the two founders chance upon an old shoe factory in the Harz mountains where they discover wooden soles from the seventies – twenty years old, never used and providing inspiration for both the craftsman and the shoe designer, these soles were taken back to Oehler's Kreuzberg workshop, where they were the subjects of much trial and research. Finally, a collection of about a dozen handmade wooden shoes emerged and were presented at the Galerie für Kunsthandwerk, garnering keen interest from designers and agents.

To cope with the orders, students, apprentices and young Serbian draft dodgers were recruited and trained. 20 people lived, worked and partied at the workshop, a grand total of 70 square meters within an old brewery. Oehler recalls that

> In the beginning it was good. Later, when the company was growing, it became more difficult since we couldn't be in the factory all the time. We needed professional workers and this was the time we went to East Germany and there was an old shoe factory and we started work there.

Its origins make for a compelling story. Today, Trippen is a business with its own full-fledged production facilities straddling Berlin and various workshops in Italy. In its German factory, located at Zehdenick, just outside Berlin, the staff strength numbers over 75, with a new extension added in 2009. True to its commitment to environmental friendliness, sustainability and social responsibility, the company supports local production: the proximity of the Zehdenick premises to Berlin transport to a minimum while creating jobs in an area with very little infrastructure. Small family businesses in Northern Italy supplement the remaining manufacturing needs.

This chapter provides a glimpse, as if through a looking glass, into the production aspects of the shoemaking company. From the operation of heavy machinery for vulcanisation to the handling of bales of leather for tanning; from the handcrafted aspect of nailing wooden shoes individually by hand to the delicate work of sewing the uppers and, for some designs, braiding leather strips by hand, the making of a shoe requires the collaborative efforts of separate teams of people with specific expertise. From the staff at the tanneries to the skilled workers who work on the various aspects of rubber or wooden sole production, *Through The Looking Glass* presents the people who stand behind the product.

Putting soles into place

PRODUCTION

Leather

Wood

Rubber

Locations

Leather

Conserved raw hides at a tannery.

In the little Tuscan town of Santa Croce, tanneries still exist, about a thousand of them, just as it has been for generations. When they started moving to the outskirts in the 1970s, nobody could have guessed that just thirty years later a much more consequential shift would be under way. Today, everything is shipped abroad: machines, personnel, know-how. Only a few Italian tanneries will survive this process. Modern chemicals have slashed the production time from two or three years down to just a few days, but it is still heavy work with the big hides on the machines, an unbearable stench and in permanently wet surroundings.

Clockwise from bottom left Checking the leather as part of quality control; Part of the leather-tanning process; Staff member at the tannery.

Wood

In 1991, the discovery by Oehler and
Spieth of some unused wooden soles
dating from the 1970s provided the
inspiration for the first ever Trippen
wooden shoes. Since then, the collection
of wooden clogs, a combination of
traditional craftsmanship and modern
design, has grown steadily. Trippen now
has about 200 designs using 40 different
wooden soles; Zen, in particular, has
been a perennial bestseller. Sourced
from various parts of Europe, the timber
is assessed for its individual type and
characteristic, crafted into unique soles
and combined with leather patterns to
create shoe sculptures.

Staff member cutting blanks.

Raw material in planks.

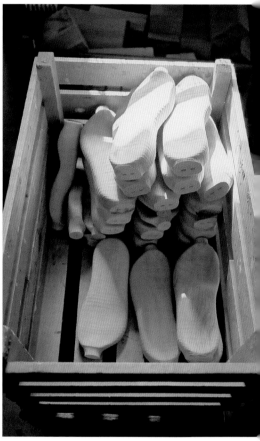

Left   Staff member sanding blanks.

Right   Blanks almost ready for use.

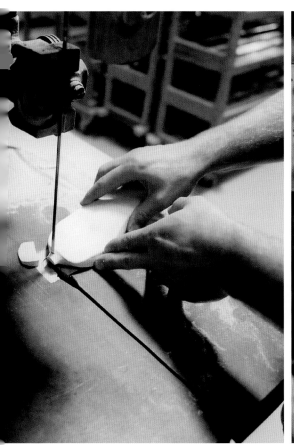

Left   Staff member cutting off excess material.

Right   Machine shaping wood.

Rubber

Trippen's soles pay particular attention
to longevity of the shoes and an
environmentally friendly use of resources.
Rubber proved the best candidate for a
material, for its recyclable nature, durable
and elastic qualities and versatility
when it comes to design. Trippen soles
are sewed, rather than glued (a widely
practiced method in the industry), onto
the upper using a patented technique that
allows worn soles to be removed, recycled
and replaced.

The rubber factory.

Facing page Aluminium moulds.

Clockwise from top left Mixing rubber colours; Raw
rubber block; Rubber after vulcanisation.

Locations

Italy

Trippen supports a local production. In Italy all manufacture takes place in small family businesses. After a series of setbacks, Trippen was able to begin working together with a family business in Northern Italy in 1995, and in the meantime a proper network of businesses – from the very small to the somewhat larger – has developed.

Staff member sanding edges.

Staff members closing uppers.

Top and bottom right
Matching pairs.

Bottom left
Staff member with
finished uppers.

Clockwise from top
Sewing the first sole seam; Cutting knives; Staff member skiving leather.

177

Locations
Zehdenick

In 1991, Michael Oehler bought some
machines from a bankrupt shoe factory
in Zehdenick near Berlin – one of many
East German state-run enterprises forced
to close after reunification. Trippen
opened its first production facility
there in 1998, initially with four former
employees of the shoe factory. As the
order books filled, Trippen established its
own manufacturing facility, developing
new products and assisting Italian
workshops. Its share of production is
growing steadily. Now there are over
seventy-five workers in Zehdenick, and
the production facilities were extended
by a modern new building in 2009.

Left Liners for the Kids collection.

Right Cutting uppers.

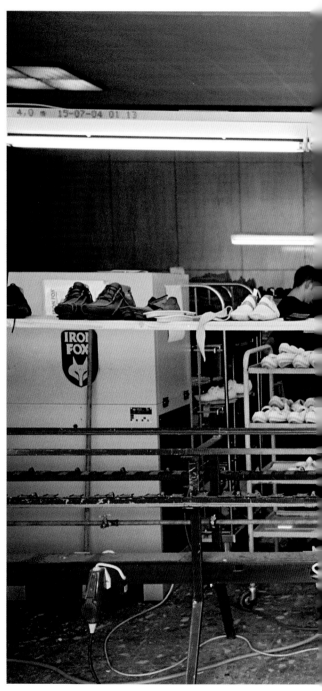

Left   "Countdown to the summer holidays".

Right   Part of the production line.

THE
SHOE-
MAKERS

Interview: Angela Spieth and Michael Oehler

How is provenance important to Trippen?

Angela We maintain the German spirit of austere, high quality products married with excellent service. We follow the Bauhaus tradition of form following function. Our priority is shorter transport routes as it saves energy. Proximity to production is essential in order to guarantee flexibility and faster delivery times. In an era where trends change quickly and up to 30 collections a year are launched, customers favour very late order deadlines so that they can purchase the best possible shoe. In order to cater to Trippen's diverse range of markets, each model is produced using a large number of different colour and material combinations. Logistically speaking, it would be far too complicated to produce these small amounts in low-wage countries. In addition, turning to local production would necessarily mean revealing our internally developed expertise. End consumers continue to value the "Made in Germany" or "Made in Italy" labels from a specific price level upwards – they still stand for extremely good quality.

Michael We were brought up in the shadow of the Bauhaus teachings, our parents purchased traditional products, we studied at academies which succeeded the Bauhaus, and, after we had striven to do everything differently and better, we realised that we had gone full circle and returned to the Bauhaus rules. This development is a cycle possible only in Europe, since its where the rules originated.

What is the process from inspiration to the finished product?

Michael It all starts with an idea, a function, a line. Afterwards, the creative frenzy begins; the idea comes to life in small sketches, projected onto the lasts and removed as a pattern before being cut out of leather and sewn together. The idea is then tweaked over the lasts, a makeshift cardboard sole is stuck underneath and the prototype is put to the test. If the idea proves its worth, the sense of happiness is immense.

Angela To continue Michael's statement, if the idea doesn't work, we pursue the development process further. This can take several seasons.

Just a century or two ago, leather was an industrial material. Today, it is almost synonymous with luxury.   How does Trippen see leather?

Michael   The majority of the leather used to make shoes is covered with a PUR layer (a layer of polyurethane soft foam), so that a unified structure is obtained and no blemishes are visible. As a result, real leather surfaces are a luxury, as nature is seldom free of flaws. In contrast, Trippen shoes show precisely where the barbed wire injured the cow or where mosquitoes plagued the elk. We often only use leather in various thicknesses in order to illustrate different functions and statements.

Angela   Trippen uses natural, traditionally tanned leather. This means that no covering PUR or protective colour layer conceals the skins' irregularities. The skins are not stamped. We use only premium, highly-priced raw materials in order to ensure that we offer our customers high-quality leather. Our cows and calves come from France, Denmark and Switzerland, as animals from other regions have too many injuries. The skins are bled out before being waxed, which allows the shoes to age attractively if cared for well. If we require specific textures or leather looks, we search for animals with interesting surface textures. Here, the texture and characteristics of buffalo (very robust) or elk (very elastic) are particularly popular.

Many of the shoemakers in Europe today are inheritors of a line of traditional shoemakers. Where is Trippen located in this age-old shoemaking tradition?

Michael   We come from two different directions: the bespoke shoemaker who has produced bespoke shoes for film and stage for a decade, and the fashion designer who has experience of the global mass market. However, both of us are completely in awe of the traditional craft. We were able to share this admiration through the medium of patternmaking, and develop it further together.

Angela At the beginning, like Michael, basic shoemaking techniques originate in Italy, Hungary and Germany. We make every effort to preserve this knowledge. These traditional production methods form the technical basis for Trippen's new developments.

How has the character of the city of Berlin influenced the character of the company?

Michael Berlin is a very free city, the legacy of the West Berlin enclave, which provided a safe haven for conscientious objectors, artists and homosexuals from the emergent FRG (Federal Republic of Germany), finally embracing the long-neglected East Berlin after the economic failure of the GDR (German Democratic Republic). Our designs reflect this freedom.

Angela Berlin has always been a city with very low rental charges. This makes it easy to found alternative companies, and there's a lot of space for creative people. This environment is very inspiring. Berlin is a very green city, but by no means an economic metropolis, and the low wage level reflects this. There is a wealth of temporary employees, but well-trained specialists are thin on the ground. This is another reason why we decided to locate our factory in Zehdenick, 70 km north of Berlin, as this was the site of a shoe factory in the GDR era, and we were able to take over several of its female workers.

How is the current economic climate influencing the brand?

Michael Trippen shoes have always been difficult to sell, as love at first sight is the exception to the rule.

Do you mean that falling in love at first sight of a Trippen shoe is rare?

Michael Yes. In the crisis, consumers are looking for sturdy, robust products. Design, comfort, materiality, ecological and social aspects – it all has to add up.

Angela The economic crisis doesn't really affect Trippen, as it has always been a niche product. Businesses which have consistently featured Trippen shoes in their product ranges are now enjoying pleasing sales. In these times of crisis, the end consumer is looking for something special, and this is where the Trippen concept bears fruit, thanks to its independent design, premium quality, high functionality and comfort at realistic prices.

What is Trippen's biggest asset?

Angela Trippen's biggest asset is its collections, which are constantly renewed and enhanced. This is not only a task for the designers, but for the whole team: the technical development, the corporate communications department, the sales department, the material and production planning, the staff in the production, the accounts department – they all fit together. That way a gesamtkunstwerk, a total work of art, emerges. This whole process is what drives Trippen's mission and is materialised in the collections. Sustainability and social responsibility are in-house values that form the basis for the process - supervised in perfectionist manner and in the responsibility of the designers. All necessary expenditures are taken to further develop this process and thus enhance the value of the gesamtkunstwerk. Beyond that, all is handed down to the consumer. As a result, the shoes do cost more than mass-produced articles, but considerably less than comparable design products.

What is in store for Trippen both in the foreseeable as well as the distant future?

Michael We will continue to design shoes and delight in the fact that our planet provides us with an unlimited amount of inspiration.

Angela We will continue to search for the perfect shoe.

What do you think will be the fate of craft in the 21st century?

Michael It will continue in two directions; some people will carry on in the classical, centuries-old handmade craft tradition, while others will use the technical developments in order to satisfy individual niches, as designers use the Mac.

Angela Traditional craft will be valued more highly. As true handicraft (made by hand) is almost extinct and very time-consuming, and as only a few people still know how to do it, it will become a rarity and thus extremely expensive. It will become a luxury. Handcrafted products will be imitated extensively, e.g. machines will be developed in order to produce as many units as possible with replicated traces of handcrafted production. Craft will become the anti-pole of the current prevailing addiction to luxury in the form of glamorous brands whose image and allure conceal a lack of product quality.

Which is your favourite shoe and why?

Michael This changes often at the moment. Loose, because it embraces my foot like a living organ with a geometrical shape.

Angela Mars, a semicircle, and Lotus, the most extreme in terms of cutting techniques.

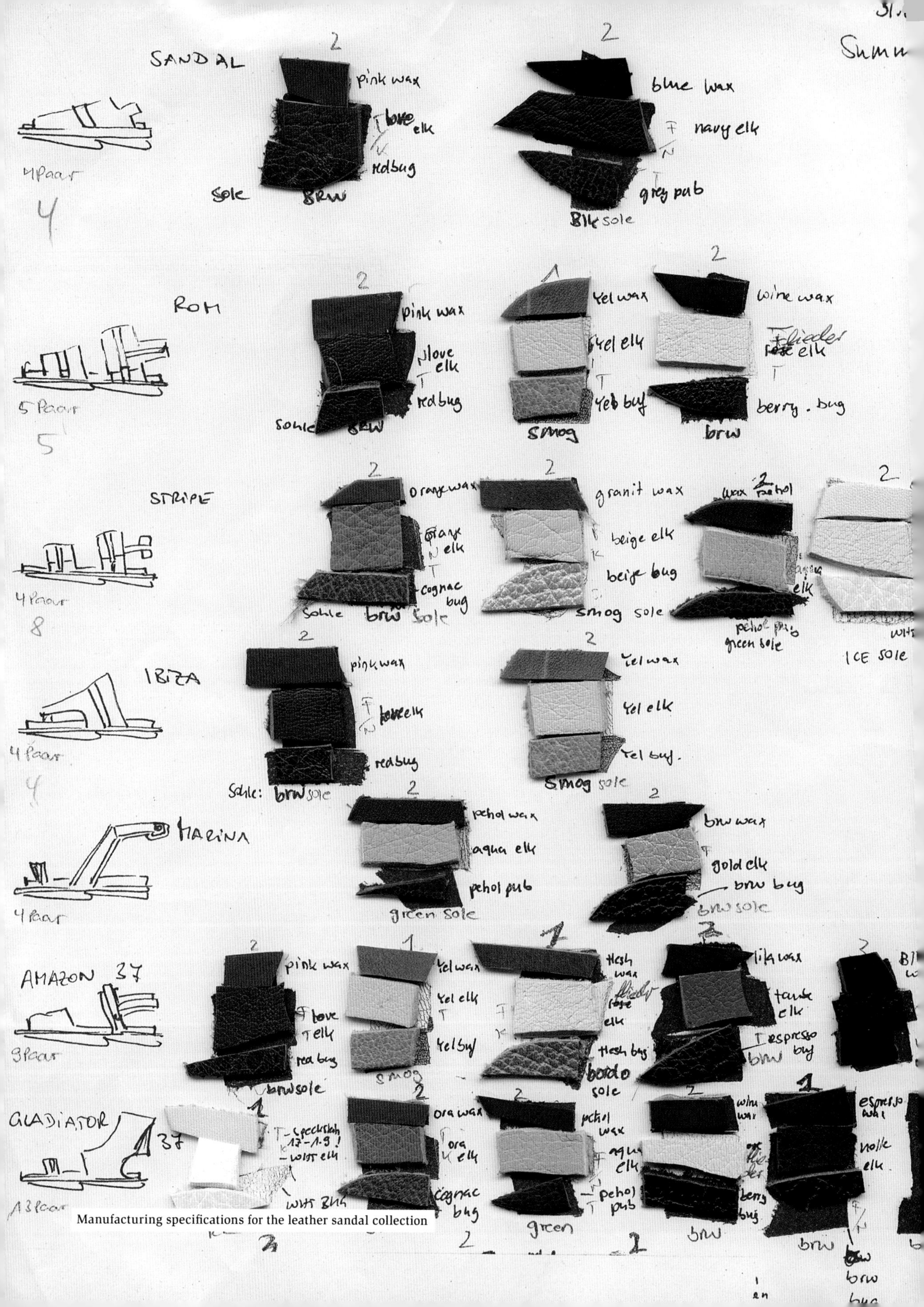

SANDAL

4 Paar

4

2 — pink wax / love elk / redbug / Sole BRW

2 — blue wax / navy elk / grey pub / Blk sole

ROM

5 Paar

5

2 — pink wax / love elk / redbug / Sohle BRW

1 — Yel wax / Yel elk / Yel bug / Smog

2 — wine wax / Flieder rose elk / berry bug / brw

STRIPE

4 Paar

8

2 — Orange wax / Orange elk / cognac bug / Sohle brw sole

2 — granit wax / beige elk / beige bug / smog sole

2 — wax petrol / elk / petrol green sole

2 — elk / WHT ICE sole

IBIZA

4 Paar

4

2 — pink wax / love elk / redbug / Sohle: brw sole

2 — Yel wax / Yel elk / Yel bug / Smog sole

MARINA

4 Paar

2 — pehol wax / aqua elk / pehol pub / green sole

2 — brw wax / gold elk / brw bug / brw sole

AMAZON 37

3 Paar

2 — pink wax / love elk / T elk / rea bug / brw sole

1 — Yel wax / Yel elk / Yel bug / smog

1 — flesh wax / Flieder rose elk / flesh bug / bordo sole

2 — lila wax / tank elk / espresso brw bug / Blk

GLADIATOR 37

A 3 Paar

1 — speckhah whit elk / WHT BH

2 — Ora wax / Ora elk / cognac bug / green

2 — pehol wax / aqua elk / pehol pub / brw

1 — espresso wax / violle elk / berry bug / brw

Manufacturing specifications for the leather sandal collection

SKETCHES

Initial Sketches

Collection Sketches

Colourways

Initial Sketches

The earliest sketches of a product often provide a fascinating peek at the inner workings of the designer's mind. From the tabula rasa of a sketchbook, an idea takes shape, evolves and, if the designer is lucky, is eventually brought to life. This section comes complete with coffee stains and crumpled hotel stationery, proof that inspiration can indeed strike at 3am.

A drawing is simply a line going for a walk.

-- Paul Klee

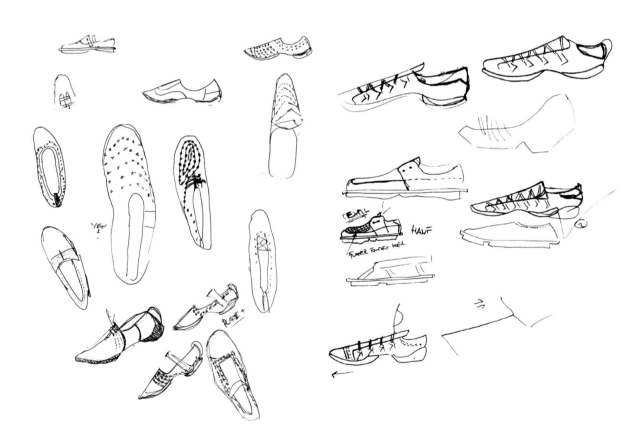

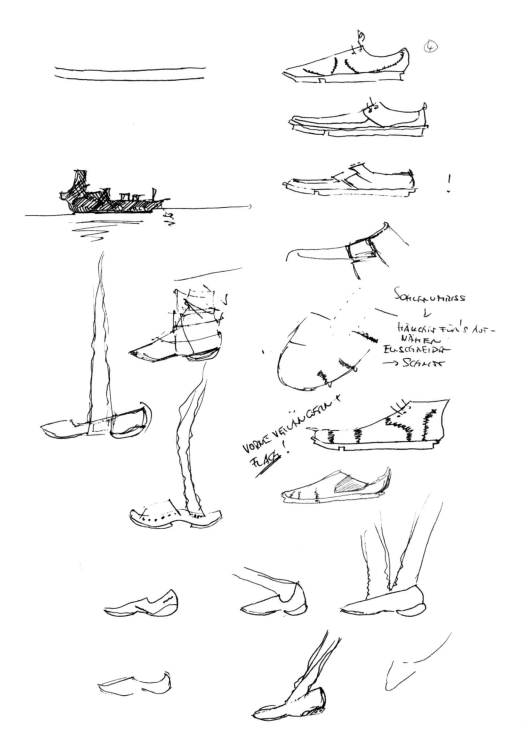

SOHLENUMRISS
↓
HÄUCHEN FÜR'S AUT-
NÄHEN
EINSCHNEIDEN
→ SCHNITT

VORNE VERLÄNGERN +
FLACH!

twin brothers
Summer rain

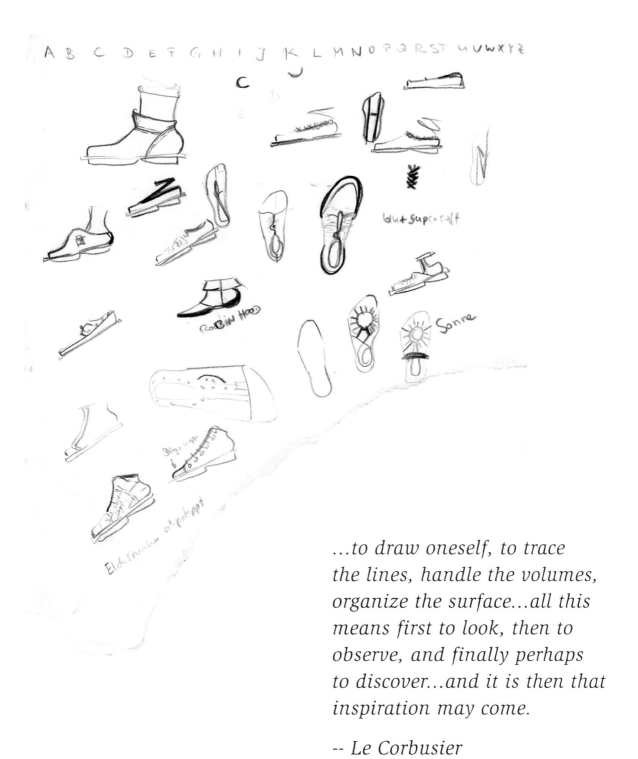

…to draw oneself, to trace the lines, handle the volumes, organize the surface…all this means first to look, then to observe, and finally perhaps to discover…and it is then that inspiration may come.

-- Le Corbusier

Collection Sketches

A unique look at the Trippen collections,
this section showcases the shoes as
sketched by the designers. Almost
prettier than the real thing, the sketches
are instantly recognisable since almost
every shoe has a distinctive silhouette.
For this reason the delicate drawings
are also used on order sheets for easy
identification by retailers. They also serve
to showcase the wide variety of styles
within each collection, a factor that
remains one of the key elements for the
brand's success.

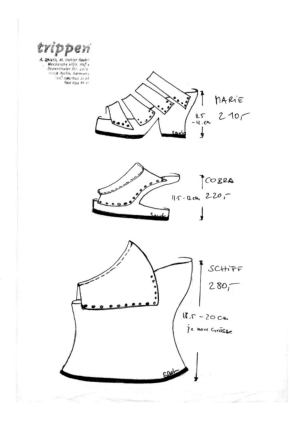

HOLZ 99

trippen
A.Spieth, M.Oehler

 JOY

 BONE

 BATMAN

 HEXE

 MEDEA

 ROHR

 UNDINE

 COBRA

 HOPPER

 MEDUSE

 SALOME

 WELLE

 HORN

 MOND

 SATURN

 ZELT

 CALLAS

 INDIA

 OLYMPIA

 SIRENE

 ZEN

 CROWN

 KREIS

 ORION

 SONNE

 PUCK

 COCO

 DIETRICH

 LIESE

 PAX

 SPANGE

 ZETT

 ERIK

 LUX

 PULSAR

 STRAHL

 GEORGE

 GAS

 MARIE

 RON

 TREPPE

 GILBERT

trippen, A.Spieth, M.Oehler GmbH, Chausseestrasse 35, 10 115 Berlin, Germany, Tel (49) 30-2807518, Fax (49) 30 - 2807517,
UST-Identnr: DE 172848929, Geschäftsführer: Angela Spieth, Michael Oehler, HRB 55048, Amtsgericht Berlin-Charlottenburg
Berliner Sparkasse BLZ 100 500 00 KTO 0610024329, Postgiroamt Berlin BLZ 100 100 10 KTO 610782102

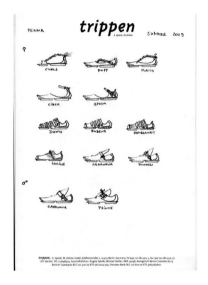

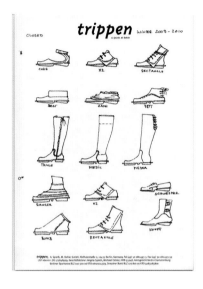

196

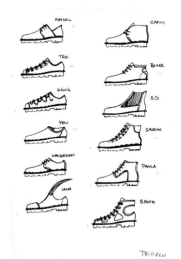

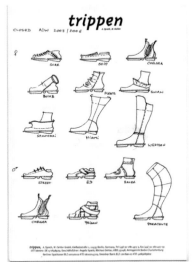

Colourways

Whether as coloured pencil drawings,
Pantone chips or actual leather samples
(from the palest of white on shiny
buffalo to the glimmer of gold on
elk), sample colours shortlisted for a
collection help the designers visualise
how the final product will turn out
before making the prototypes, finalising
the patterns, cutting the uppers, and
creating the final sample collections.

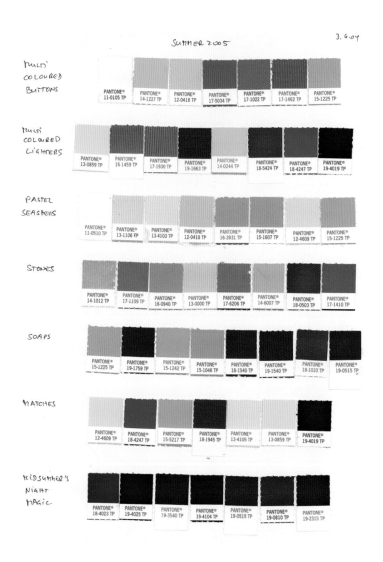

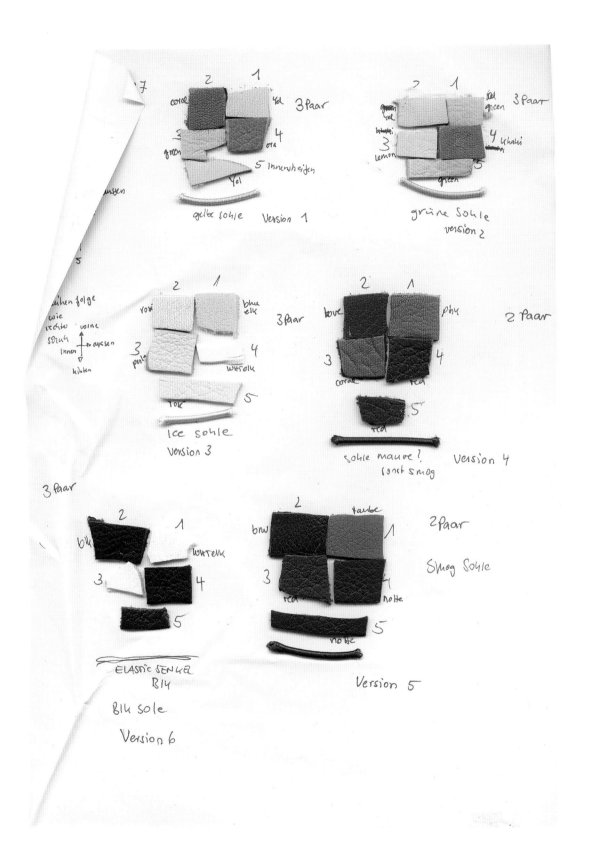

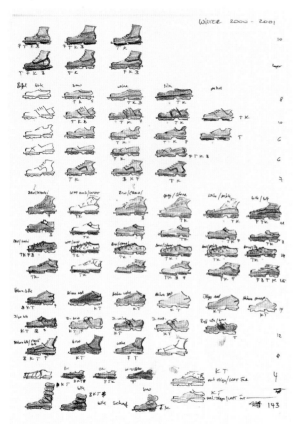

WINTER 2000 - 2001

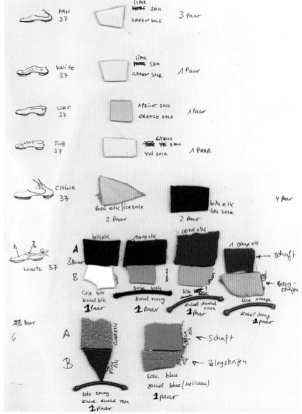

200

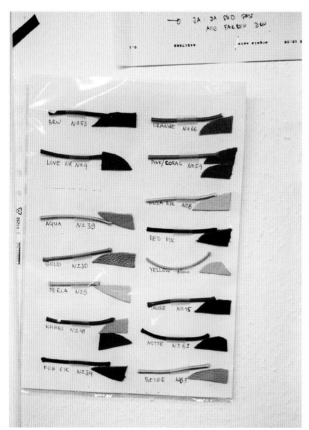

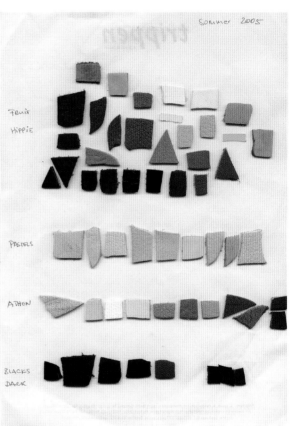

*You reason color more than
you reason drawing... Color
has a logic as severe as form.*

-- Pierre Bonnard

Tools of the trade – shoe lasts and leather samples

TRIPPEN'S TRIPS

———————

Trippen's advertisements in popular magazines Wallpaper, i-D and Dazed &
Confused are unusually wordy. The chunks of text sit next to the already curious-
looking shoes. On closer inspection, other unconventional things surface: the shoes
are described as "thoughtful", "non-wearable" and "courageous", which sound
like euphemisms for less than fine design. Instead of witty, showy text boasting its
range of dazzling colours, or its popularity amongst celebrities, there is explanation
on shock-absorbing properties, pre-moulded insoles and how virgin wood soles
allow the foot to "breathe freely".

In truth, these advertisements from 2000 were the only ones ever taken out by the
company. Herein lies one of the biggest differences between Trippen and its rivals: it
eschews advertising of the brand and is rooted in the belief that advertisements do
not add real knowledge of the brand for the consumer, the way seeing the production
workers at work cutting patterns, skiving, stitching, gluing uppers, lasting, nailing
wooden soles, or braiding leather strips does. The philosophy obviously also has
effects on costs and pricing policies. Oehler explains that he wanted the company's
operations to be:

> ... simple, clear and direct. ... We didn't want to sell (our products) for a higher
> price to accommodate a marketing budget. We wanted a product that always speaks
> for itself, and what people pay for is no more than what the product is worth. This
> concept is antique, from the '50s... but it still works...

Trippen's Trips opens with the only three full-fledged advertisements they have ever
made, and then presents the array of postcards produced as invitations to trade fairs,
seasonal collections, showcases, workshops and shop openings. These postcards
echo the sensibilities behind the shoes themselves by first being fully functional
collateral, and then by marrying a consistently strong design concept with a mix
of tones depending on the current collection: often industrial (gritty black-and-

white close-ups of textured material for autumn/winter 2006/07), sometimes coolly enigmatic (an empty snow-covered sidewalk for winter 2004/05) and at least once, plain cheerful (a crowded shoreline dotted by pops of colour from the sunbathers for summer 2009).

Like the advertisements, there is a clear aversion to ornamentation without purpose, or form without function. The cover of the autumn/winter 2009/2010 catalogue is another good example of this approach: a shot of a fully-loaded container ship on the high seas, and apart from the Trippen logo, not much else. At first glance, this seems incongruous, even peculiar. The riddle is solved upon introduction to this season's star collections; the container boxes seem to allude to Box and Happy, with the shoes' boxy, cuboid platform rubber soles. Part of the wording on the container ship spells "yun", the Chinese word for transportation, suggesting goods mass-produced and shipped from the low-wage manufacturing giant – a giant Trippen refuses to turn to in their pursuit of high product quality and fair wages.

Fashion labels have turned to Trippen for shoots and runway shows. These include Cooperative Designs from London and Moon Young Hee from Paris. Of special mention is a collaboration with Issey Miyake that began in 2003. Outside of fashion, Trippen also participated at the Le Berlin des Créateurs in Paris, a 2007 exhibition focused on Berlin-based, independent and non-mainstream designers, thus underlining Trippen's affiliation to the city's design scene.

The chapter, and this book, closes with the retail arm of the brand. Other than its locations in Berlin and the rest of Germany, Trippen has also made the retail markets of Japan (Daikanyama, Harajuku, Kobe and Nagoya), Israel (Tel Aviv), Spain (Bilbao), Taiwan (Taipei and Taichung) and London its playground. Steering clear of excessive advertisement and stripping down to bare essentials, focusing on sound design spiked with a dash of spunk and irony, Trippen brings the heart of the business back to the basics, of what a piece of work is a shoe. The shoes come first, and all media, events, even the stores, centre on it, not the other way round.

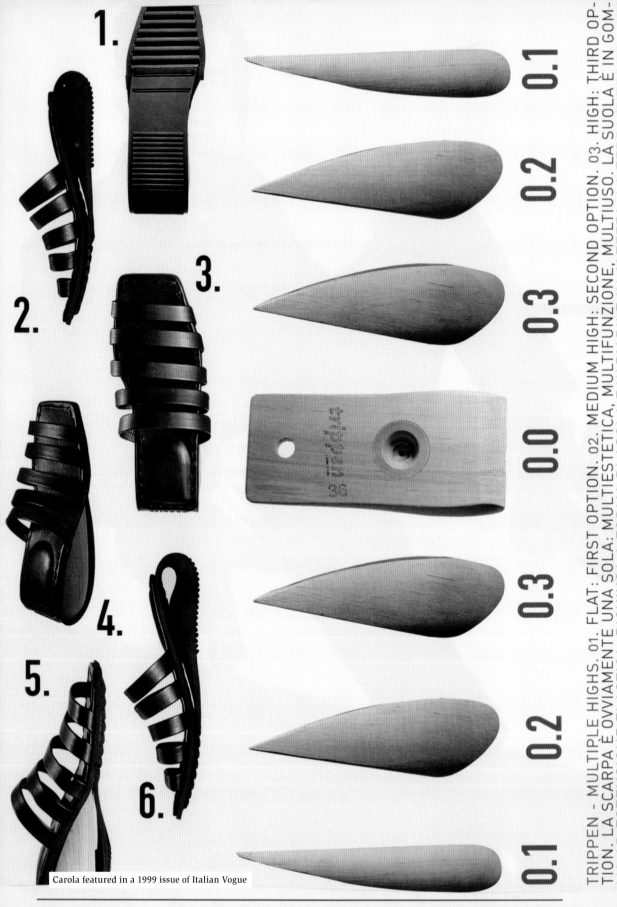

1.

2.

3.

4.

5.

6.

0.1

0.2

0.3

0.0

0.3

0.2

0.1

Carola featured in a 1999 issue of Italian Vogue

TRIPPEN - MULTIPLE HIGHS. 01. FLAT: FIRST OPTION. 02. MEDIUM HIGH: SECOND OPTION. 03. HIGH: THIRD OPTION. LA SCARPA È OVVIAMENTE UNA SOLA: MULTIESTETICA, MULTIFUNZIONE, MULTIUSO. LA SUOLA È IN GOMMA AD ESTENSIONE ELASTICA, RICHIUSA A FORMA DI ASOLA E VARIABILE IN ALTEZZA. LA ZEPPA INTERNA - UN ROCCHETTO DI LEGNO NATURALE - È INFATTI ASPORTABILE E SOSTITUIBILE A SCELTA. LA TOMAIA DI QUESTO SANDALO È IN CUOIO A LISTINI E AVVOLGE MORBIDAMENTE IL PIEDE DAL COLLO DELL'ALLUCE AL COLLO DEL PIEDE

MEDIA &
COLLATERAL

Advertisements

- - - - - -

Postcards

- - - - - -

Promotional Material

- - - - - -

Fashion Shoots

- - - - - -

Exhibitions and Shows

Advertisements

Shoes that express an individuality not found in the traditional mass market. Shoes that when hand made, would be simply too expensive to afford. trippen's interest lies in the constant movement towards designing innovative, thoughtful and endurable shoes. Endurable not only with regard to quality but durability within the rapidly changing face of fashion. Through unique cuts, simple forms and recognisable silhouettes, that have become like a trademark, trippen has managed to outlive whims and trends to establish its own niche within the industry. Designs that range from the classical to the avantgarde to the simply courageous. Shoes that stand the test of time to develop into classics. In 1992 while pottering around an old lasts factory, they discovered wood soles from the Seventies, this proved to be the inspiration that would start the adventure trippen. The first trippen collection was presented in a Berlin art gallery and consisted of 60 wearable and non-wearable wooden shoes.

trippen-holz: native woods are moulded into unusual shaped soles. It's the wood in this virgin form, in combination with the thick natural leather, that makes the shoes so comfortable to wear. The leather gradually takes on the individual form of the foot, while the natural wood allows the foot to breathe freely.

trippen-closed: what gives the trippen closed their uniqueness is their slick design and original silhouettes. The removeable rubbersole is specially developed to provide maximal flexibility and shock absorbtion. Old soles can be easily removed for recycling and new soles easily sewn on. The exchangeable premoulded insoles enhance the comfort for the wearer, as all leather that comes into contact with the foot is treated only with natural products. The appeal of the basic collection is that of simplicity and durability. The nature of the leather used is what has helped to create the trippen 'look'. The more the shoes are worn, the more their individual character comes into form.

shop: 55 Neal Street, London WC2
tel: 0207 497 0534

trippen
A. Spieth, M. Oehler

www.trippen-shoes.com

Advertisement taken out in several issues of Dazed & Confused magazine, summer 2000.

Shoes that express an individuality not found in the traditional mass market. Shoes that when hand made, would be simply too expensive to afford.

trippen's interest lies in the constant movement towards designing innovative, thoughtful and endurable shoes. Endurable not only with regard to quality but durability within the rapidly changing face of fashion. Through unique cuts, simple forms and recognisable silhouettes, that have become like a trademark, trippen has managed to outlive whims and trends to establish its own niche within the industry. Designs that range from the classical to the avantgarde to the simply courageous. Shoes that stand the test of time to develop into classics. In 1992 while pottering around an old lasts factory, they discovered wood soles from the Seventies, this proved to be the inspiration that would start the adventure trippen. The first trippen collection was presented in a Berlin art gallery and consisted of 60 wearable and non-wearable wooden shoes.

trippen-holz: native woods are moulded into unusual shaped soles. It's the wood in this virgin form, in combination with the thick natural leather, that makes the shoes so comfortable to wear. The leather gradually takes on the individual form of the foot, while the natural wood allows the foot to breathe freely.

trippen-closed: what gives the trippen closed their uniqueness is their slick design and original silhouettes. The removeable rubbersole is specially developed to provide maximal flexibility and shock absorbtion. Old soles can be easily removed for recycling and new soles easily sewn on. The exchangeable premoulded insoles enhance the comfort for the wearer, as all leather that comes into contact with the foot is treated only with natural products. The appeal of the basic collection is that of simplicity and durability. The nature of the leather used is what has helped to create the trippen 'look'. The more the shoes are worn, the more their individual character comes into form.

shop: 55 Neal Street, London WC2

www.trippen-shoes.com | tel: 0207 497 0534

trippen
A. Spieth, M. Oehler

Postcards

trippen

Einladung zur Eröffnung

workshop
10.-15. October 1996
Samaritaine Department Store
Shop No 1 (toys), Door 77
77, Rue de Rivoli
75001 Paris

trippen

trippen

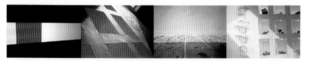

grand opening 7.7.2000

Top Invitation to the opening of the Trippen Gallery store in Alte Schönhauser Strasse on Friday, 13 December 2002, with presentation of the Cup collection.

Middle Invitation to Workshop, a trade fair called held at the Samaritaine Department Store in Paris in October 1996, showcasing the spring/summer collection 1997.

Bottom Invitation to grand opening of the extended Trippen flagship store in Hackesche Höfe in July 2000.

REPTILIEN
AUTUMN WINTER 06 07

trippen

trippen

trippen

winter 2004/2005

Top   Trade fair invitation to view the autumn/winter 2006/2007 collections.

Middle   Trade fair invitation to view the autumn/winter 2007/2008 collections.

Bottom   Trade fair invitation to view the autumn/winter 2004/2005 collections.

**Summer
06**

trippen

trippen

Facing page Trade fair invitation to view the spring/summer 2009 collections.

Left Trade fair invitation to view the spring/ summer 2006 collections.

Right Trade fair invitation to view the autumn/ winter 2005/2006 collections.

trippen

Promotional postcard.

Facing page

Top   Trade fair invitation to view the spring/ summer 2007 collections.

Bottom   Invitation to the opening party of the Trippen store in Heidelberg on 22 August 2008.

sp

er *trippen* **printemps** été **frühling** sommer **2007**

Eröffnung

trippen

Promotional Material

Brochure in a concertina fold.

Einladung

GDS 7 G20 19.3.98- 22.3.98 Düsseldorf

Workshop 11.3.98 - 16.3.98 Paris
Samaritaine, Rue de Rivoli, 77

Trade fair invitation to the GDS in Düsseldorf and Workshop in Paris.

Promotional poster from 2006.

Promotional poster on the occasion of Trippen's 5th anniversary, spring 2000.

Fashion Shoots

This and facing page Private photo shoot for
photographer's, stylist's and model's portfolios.

This and facing page Fashion shoot for designer
Julia Knüpfer's autumn/winter 2008/2009 collection,
Living Rooms.

Fashion shoot for clothing label Lino Factory's
winter 2006 collection.

Fashion shoot for clothing label Lino Factory's
winter 2009 collection.

Left Fashion shoot for clothing label Lino Factory's winter 2009 collection.

Bottom left, middle and right Fashion shoot for clothing label Lino Factory's summer 2009 collection.

Part of fashion spread published in the September 2007 issue of *Made 05*, a fashion, art and design magazine.

2008 fashion shoot for Berlin-based
designer Helena Ruff.

Exhibitions and Shows

Le Berlin des Créateurs
(The Berlin Creators)

In the autumn of 2007, Paris and Berlin came together to celebrate the 20th anniversary of the cultural co-operation agreement between the two capitals. Among the wealth of projects which included concerts and presentations of guest artists, each partner city mounted parallel exhibitions as tribute to the arts scene of the other. At the Märkisches Museum in Berlin, Design Reference Paris showcased a panorama of Parisian design from 20 September to 4 November. Meanwhile, Paris presented the Le Berlin des Créateurs, which provided a comprehensive overview of the Berlin design scene and its latest trends. Held at the VIA (Valorisation de l'Innovation dans l'Ameublement) Gallery from 3 October to 16 December, the exhibition included a showcase of Trippen shoes.

Le Berlin des Créateurs was mounted by Kulturprojekte Berlin GmbH, commissioned by the city state of Berlin and supported by the Deutsche Klassenlotterie foundation. Industrial and fashion designers, who formed the core of the show, showed off the creative stimulation brought about by the political and economic situation in Berlin and its impact on young artists and designers. Years of industrial regression (in West Berlin before the fall of the Berlin Wall, and the city in general after that) have forced designers to look beyond the expectations and needs of industry players. This questioning of design focused on industrial imperatives has fostered a new creative culture almost devoid of commercial bias.

The exhibition proposed a context of constant change and movement, representative of the initiatives and attitudes of the players in the Berlin design scene. Defying rules and conventions, they challenged established norms and confronted the expectations of the public in an attempt to imagine the future together. On display were giant screens with a series of photo portraits of creators and impressions of their work spaces by photographer Jan Sobottka. Accompanying the exhibition was an 80-page magazine with articles documenting the design and culture scene in the German city.

The team behind Kulturprojekte Berlin GmbH – Thomas Friedrich, Kathrin Kohle, Wolf Kuhnelt, Georg von Wilcken – worked alongside a group of academic experts to select 19 design agencies and fashion studios for the exhibition. The latter group included Atilano Gonzalez, Designmai, Professors Ralf Rautenberg and Helmut Staubach of the Kunsthochschule Weißensee, Professors Egon Chemaitis and Valeska Schmidt-Thomsen of the Universität der Künste in Berlin.

Industrial designers and studios who were eventually picked for the show included Adam und Harborth, Studio Aisslinger, Julian Appelius, Delphin-Design, e27, Fuchs und Funke, Hering Berlin, L.ufer und Keichel, Metrofarm, Osko und Deichmann and Barbara Schmidt (Kahla Porzellan). Other than Trippen GmbH, the fashion labels participating included Bless Office Berlin, c.neeon, Elena Kikina, Frank Leder, Pulver Studio, Karen Scholz und Joan Tarrag and Pampanola.

Left and right GDS trade fair, Düsseldorf, year unknown.

Facing page CPD trade fair, Düsseldorf, year unknown.

Clockwise from top left Trippen's 3rd participation in the GDS trade fair, Düsseldorf, 1995; Trippen shoes at the their 2nd participation in the GDS trade fair, Düsseldorf; Trippen sales team and friends in a Düsseldorf bar after the GDS trade fair, year unknown.

The Trippen stand at the CIFF trade fair, Copenhagen, 2008.

Trippen flagship store at Hackesche Höfe, Berlin

STORES

Germany

Berlin

Germany
Cologne

Germany
Heidelberg

Iceland

Reykjavik

Trippen's presence in the Icelandic capital city. The store has since closed.

Japan
Daikanyama, Kobe, Nagoya

The store in Kobe at the top and its counterpart in Nagoya at the bottom.

The store in Daikanyama.

Taiwan
Taichung, Taipei

Trippen's presence in Taipei above, and in Taichung on the facing page.

United Kingdom
London

Left and right   The first Trippen store in London, which has since closed.

FOOT NOTES: AN INDEX OF SHOE MODELS

Pieces of uppers cut out

Shelf with spools of thread

CREDITS